# OPERATION BIG FUN: THE FEST LIFE GUIDE

## By Suzanne Wentley

ISBN: 978-0-692-12108-5

Dedicated to my *framily*,
all the beautiful people
I've met along my musical path

# Table of Contents

**Above, lights, rage sticks, parachute shade art installation, music, friends: Operation Big Fun in full effect. Now go on and get in the middle of that crowd!**

**Cover photo: Detail of the Further Bus, as displayed at The Gorge in George, Washington. Cover design by Tara Biek.**

All photos in this guide were taken by Suzanne Wentley, or a kindly random friend who happened to be passing by, except where otherwise noted. We love everyone in these pictures and you for looking at them and buying this guide. Please use with caution and hang on.  E pluribus unum. Om.

# INTRODUCTION

Live music festivals exist in a magical place and time, where the worries of normal life can slip away and be replaced by belly laughter and carefree dancing. You fall asleep smiling and awake refreshed and cozy under a canopy of shady trees, ready for another day of adventure. You experience new music, meet new friends and create fun, colorful memories that buoy you during the most stressful days of work and responsibility. Festivals remind you of the good in life and can leave a ***perma-grin*** on your face.

*Or* ... your tent breaks. Your dirtbag neighbors steal your favorite bike. You miss the awesome band everyone was talking about. You spend too much money and are cold (or hot), hungry and exhausted. You fight with your significant other. You get super-sick. You start to think you're too old for this shit.

Which version would you prefer? (*Editor Interjection*: *Look, you don't have to answer that.)*

This guide is designed to help you master The Fest Life. We're ***happy to help*** you have the best time of your life.

Music festivals are more than just about the music. They are about letting your hair down and shaking off the parts of life that dull your inner love light. It's simply about having fun. When that happens, you feel free. When it doesn't, well, you don't.

It may not feel like it at the time, but which experience you have is your choice and your choice alone. It's not just attitude (although it's a lot of that). Having an amazing, unforgettable time at a music festival is also a matter of skill, experience and wisdom. The fact that you're reading this means you're serious about having fun and ready for more. Congratulations!

We bought a great bumper sticker and slapped it on the back of an ex-boyfriend's car. It reads: ***If you're having fun, you're doing it right.*** Let's do it right, people.

Each year, hundreds of thousands of people buy a pricey ticket to a live music festival in those warm, beautiful months each year when organizers create dream line-ups of popular bands in venues (sometimes) designed for an onslaught of the masses. Young, hip and happy people (or at least relatively so) pack their cars filled with stuff and are stoked to sport a colorful wristband all weekend. Some people refuse to take those wristbands off for months, until they get really dirty and gross and their moms are embarrassed for them.

We'll discuss this phenomenon, by the way, along with all the rest. Unsure of what the heck we are talking about sometimes? This guide has come equipped with a glossary (*Edit: We hyper-linked for the e-books but, dear paperback-reading dinosaur, you have use your thumbs to flip yourself.)* Vocabulary words and phrases are *italicized* AND *emboldened* for your studying pleasure – and you will be quizzed. This glossary has resulted in much foot-dragging on our part to write but contains the basic definitions of many highlighted words and phrases found throughout this guide. You have to speak the language, or at least our strange version of the language, to maximize the Fest Life. Feel free to sprinkle these phrases during your next cocktail and, if you're living in one of the enlightened states, marijuana party. As part of our likely non-existent marketing campaign for this guide, we have hired young, cool ground teams in media-soaked cities to spread our glossary terms on the streets like wildfire. So consider yourself on the ground floor. *#yourewelcome*. ***#sorrynotsorry***!

Ah, the Fest Life! Ain't it grand? We're sure by now you've been to a music festival, yes? Which ridiculously named event did you go to? Bonnaroo, Langerado, Wanee, Coachella ... the fact that most of these fest names aren't even real words suggest a creativity and opportunity to leave the real world behind and make your own reality. There's something really special about that.

But the vast majority of people aren't going at all ... or simply fail at maximizing the magic for a simple reason: They aren't prepared for the ***new reality*** of live music festivals. Get a random sample of folks who have shelled out a couple hundred dollars for a fest. A handful will be wide-eyed and dripping with superlatives about how life-changing the weekend was for them. They swear they will go to the same festival every year. And some do! We once met a couple who got married at the first Lock'n Festival in Virginia and had the festival logo (a broken sideways figure 8 infinity symbol, which is kind of cool, we guess, for a logo) tattooed to their calves. It felt both long- and short-sighted, frankly.

**Left, speaking of Frank (and Lynn!), meet a couple of friends who got engaged at a Wanee Festival and wed right before the Lock'n Festival, where we met up for big hugs in the crowd**

Still, many people who go to a music festival will never go again, mostly because they just really didn't know how to enjoy the adventure. They were just plain wiped out upon their return home. They feel like, once and done. But if you only experience these wonderful worlds once, we're here to tell you, you're not reaching the heights you deserve.

We've been a regular at music festivals for more than a decade, with many friends going a lot longer. At this point, you've likely noticed that we've purposefully chosen to express ourselves in the strange yet appropriate first-person plural voice, in which fellow guide writers often enjoy partaking. Because while much of the advice you'll discover and, presumably, retain through copious notes in the margins, came directly from the author's own experience, we're not alone. We're not talking about voices in our heads, because those monkeys in our mind are totally Wizard of Oz-style flying outta here – and no, that's not the last time you'll enjoy a befitting Wizard of Oz reference in this guide. The point is, we're received a crazy-amount (*Edit: Maybe we do have a little voice in our head. See what we did there?)* of input on how to make the Fest Life fabulous.

Over the last decade, we've been to lots of festivals, both small and large, near our house(s? Oh, we may regret writing in this voice) and far enough away that airplanes were, shall we say, involved. We know there are a bunch of seasoned folks reading this who have been to many more festivals and may know more than us (*Edit: As if! OK, probably.).* Our Fest experience includes: All the Wanee Festivals in Florida, plus numerous SpringFests, Magnolia Festivals, the Jazz & Heritage Festival in New Orleans (known fondly as Jazz Fest) and Orange Blossom Jamboree in the middle of Florida.

**Left, a Jam Cruise crowd listens to an acoustic set at the piano with Ivan Neville under the glittery staircases.**

We've also been to Lock'n, Gathering of the Vibes along the Long Island Sound in New York, Langerado (both in Fort Lauderdale and in the cow patty-and-fire ant haven of Big Cypress in the Everglades), on Jam Cruise originating from Miami, Grassroots Festival and the Virginia Key festival in Miami. Plus, you may have hugged us at the b.e. easy Festival in Lake Worth, the short-lived AsheFest in the beautiful Deerfields outside of Asheville, North Carolina, Sweetwater 420 in downtown Atlanta and a great camping weekend for Phish at The Gorge in Washington state that was a basically a festival without a crazy name. We swung into the Swings and Sol festival in Mexico but otherwise no other festivals outside of the United States. Nor have we been to every music festival inside the United States, but we believe the wisdom holds true internationally. We may like different music than you (*Edit: boocheeboocheeboochee*), but this is more about how to conduct yourself at a festival rather than what type of music to like.

So, we're experts, OK? We're writing a frickin' guide. It will be self-published, OK? An E-book! ***E*!** If that letter is not impressive, then you are simply not modern. If you have more tips or corrections, we would appreciate you adding them in an Amazon comment so we can sell a bunch of these guides as well as start an endless online social media debate that may or may not end in us unfriending you and wondering why you won't just leave it alone.

Some of the festivals we've attended have been challenging and some have been a dream. They were always memorable. We'll never forget the beginning of our Fest Life, the first hour of our first camping music festival. It went a little something like this:

Live oak branches and Spanish moss were tickling the top of our new, silver Volkswagen Beetle as we arrived with our redheaded best friend at the time, who was a solid yet loopy concert-going companion who also worked at the same newspaper we did. We had popped in a bootleg of a Grateful Dead concert in the CD player as we rolled into the site, following directions that led to a group of her friends who had set up camp at the first Wanee

Festival at the beautiful Spirit of the Suwannee Music Park in Live Oak, Florida. This is a venue, by the way, that should not be missed.

**Right, another shot of one of our favorite venues: The Spirit of the Suwannee Music Park in Live Oak, FL**

So Robin (*Edit: whose name, like all names and identifying hair colors in this guide, may or may not be changed to protect the awesome and/or awful, but never, ever innocent*) and we had already done some mini-tours together, seeing The Dead up in the Carolinas and Georgia, as well as traveling around Florida for the Allman Brothers and other off-shoots of the Dead, including Phil & Friends and Ratdog. We were pretty stoked to have packed up the car to drive about four hours north to the spot.

We reached the gates already pretty high, because "we" smoked a lot of reefer (*Edit: We're not going to say which if any of one of our writing team partook because: legal advice*). Upon receiving our wristbands and parking passes, we navigated our way through the bumpy, shady trails to the campsite. We had purchased our first flip-style cell phone a couple years before, (which should create an interesting sense of time) so we used this new-fangled piece of equipment to find camp, which was already set up with EZ-Up tents and folding camping chairs placed around a fire ring. I saw a tall pole, leaning against a car, topped with a plastic gray mule with an American flag painted on its side. This is known as a ***rage stick***, to be discussed later in the guide. This crew was evidently big fans of Warren Haynes' band, Gov't Mule.

We pulled in, and we immediately met Dan. Danny Boy was and remains one well-seasoned in the Fest Life. He even carried a flask with a Grateful Dead Steal Your Face on it, with the words "Fest Your Face" emblazoned on the side.

We shook hands, and his smile immediately turned serious as he looked over a furrowed brow, gravely at us.

"There are bad chocolate mushrooms going around," he said, conveying a weary look of a rough night. His eyes shifted to the side, and he took a drag off a cigarette.

"Don't eat those. It's a really bad idea," he said, shaking his head. "Trust me."

We trusted him. And we had a weekend filled with so much fun that it propelled us into a decade of dedicated festival-going, leading to so many amazing experiences we are frankly excited to share in this guide.

We've sought out and taken advice from veterans whenever we could over the years, and as a result, we've become veterans ourselves (speaking as a writing team). In fact, our friends Chris and Harry, bespectacled brothers and grinning goofballs who we think will enjoy reading this guide, cemented us as parts of the scene when, one year, they passed out small, bright orange stickers not only with the faces of our favorite New Orleans funk musicians but with faces of their friends as well.

**Right, proof of which we speak**

This little face of ours, in an even littler Girl Scout costume, was on a sticker. We were quite honored by this and use it as continued proof that you can trust us, we're always scouting the funk.

Our goal with this manual is to help our friends (and ***future friends***) make the most out of the festival experience, regardless of the number of concerts they've seen. We hope this advice will be useful (and also entertaining, even if we get in a fight later in the comments section) as the years of music festivals have added many memories – both pleasant and distinctly unpleasant – to our lives. For this writing team, represented by a *certain* person's picture in the "about the author" section (*Edit: W.T.F.*), we believe the less-than-awesome moments can be used as lessons for next time. And isn't learning, progressing and helping one another achieve awesomeness what life is all about?

If you've been to a festival, we know you'll have lots to add to this guide. In fact, you don't have to limit feedback to the comments section. How about you tell us next time you see us after a show? But only right after we ***hug hello***.

# Chapter 1: Self-Sufficiency

*"I saw you with a ticket stub in your hand!" – Phish*

There are so many music festivals organized throughout the globe – how do you decide which one to go to? For us, we hone in on a few variables:

1. Line up! The ***music is the priority***. It doesn't matter how epic a venue, how convenient a location and ideal a date, you're simply not going to go to a bluegrass festival if you're really into techno. It may seem obvious, but this is worth recognizing: The reason you are going to a music festival is to enjoy the music. That is the bottom line, and yet so easy to forget when there are so many distractions and friends and crazy-boozy nights during the festival itself. Again, music is the priority! You are going there to see live music! It's vital to arrive with the end game in mind, and that is music. You may love ***yucking*** it up

around the campfire with your friends, filling up on awesome foodstuffs and staying up all night; but you can do that without the whopping big-ticket, early-bird-if-you're-on-it entry price. Seriously, if music isn't your end game, then by all means email a few friends and pick a date for a weekend at a state park. Boom. Done. But that's not the Fest Life, now is it?

**Below, the Nouveaux Honkies play at Terra Fermata in Stuart. Not really a festival, we must admit, but a fun angle and one of the writing team *riding the rail.***

So, study the line ups of bands when all the festival dates start getting announced before jumping on any ticket purchases. ***You can't do everything***, but you might as well check a few of your favorite bands off the ole bucket list.

2. Date – You know that online virtual reality game called Second Life? We've never played it, but some friends have. One friend decided to make her avatar have a really, really big booty! That fake world may seem crazy and perhaps psychologically

unstable, but running around with fairy wings and glitter? Totally OK.

Nonetheless, just like that virtual reality game, you have to juggle the Fest Life with real life. That means when picking a festival to attend, it's vital to weigh family, professional and all other obligations. Don't make festing some excuse for not being a good father or co-worker or whatever. Plan ahead when scheduling this extreme fun in your life – chances are you'll have to ask off work and save up vacation days (*Edit: It is absolutely, 100% mandatory as a reader of this guide to use EVERY single vacation day you earn at work. You didn't see that in the fine print when you purchased this e-guide, likely in an e-book format? Well, now you e-know. Start e-planning.* ***E****!)* If you have kids, you'll have to plan for them. Few festivals are truly kid-friendly, and we'll discuss this. Maybe the squirts can have a week with your 'rents. Many festivals are during the summer holidays anyway.

Speaking of sultry summers, the date of festivals also determine the temperature of the weekend. Are you cool with cold? Think about it. We, as a collective team of independent, remotely stationed writers, are not. Otherwise we would have gone to the now-defunked (*see what we did there?)* funk odyssey that was the Bear Creek festival every November in northern Florida. We called it Brrr Creek. The calendar is an important part of real life you must consider when you fall into the fantastically fun spiral of music festivals!

3. Location! Location! Location!: Just like buying real estate, this is a major element of the magic of music festivals. So, as we are writing this, there are organizers creating a fest in Okeechobee, which is a very rural, small town at the top of a large lake in the middle of Florida. Think cow fields on low-lying, easily flooded land next to a huge lake filled with alligators and swarming with mosquitoes. This is not an ideal location. A mountaintop on the outskirts of Asheville, N.C. with sponge-y, green grass and a chilly, fresh lake WITHOUT alligators? Yes please.

Now, if you live 20 minutes from Okeechobee and hours from Asheville, your reaction may be very different. That's because location also determines logistics. How will you be arriving at said festival? It might have the most epic line-up on the one weekend you're completely free from all obligations, but if it's in Timbuktu, you're probably not going. Although, can you make it happen? Think about it! Don't be intimidated by festivals that are far away. You can get a flight and some cheap camping gear that you can also probably return after you use it at Wal-Mart (*Edit: The legal department has already reprimanded the writing team.),* grab a couple gallons of water and get your rental car right to the spot just in time for the most awesome performance by your favorite band ever. But of course, life is made so much easier if you can pack up at home and drive there with your home crew of buddies.

4. Check with the crew. Speaking of those fun-loving buds, consultation with your friends is the next step. We've attended music festivals with a variety of lovers and friends. We've also gone to fests by our lonesome, and news flash: It is not lonesome at all! In fact, we highly recommend attending a music festival by yourself. You may have find that you are your very own best friend – plus you won't have to put up with anyone else's bullshit. When's the last time you didn't have to do that? ***Just sayin'***.

Once you weigh these variables, it's time for the super-exciting biting of the bullet. Clicking the "buy" button for a music festival ticket is so fun! Yay! It is so empowering to make an executive decision and remember that: Woo-hoo! You are an adult and you get to decide what you do with your own life! That initial ***ticket high***, we must say, is pretty awesome. *(EDIT: Look, we know tickets are expensive. We'll discuss all this in Chapter 8: Making It Happen.)*

But we're here to tell you: The right line-up, date, location and crew of friends aren't the only key elements to success in ***Operation Big Fun***. You must be self-sufficient in order to have a fantastic experience. See, whether you're a total drunken dirtbag (*EDIT: The legal department wants you know* *that we are NOT talking about you. No, NO! Not you ... um, we were talking to the other reader. That guy!)* or a total ***newb*** (*EDIT: Heh, heh. Yeah, whatever!)* or somewhere in between, YOU are responsible for YOU in the end. While it's important to help your brothers and sisters (see *Chapter 4: Finding a Friend in Everyone*), you are making a pact with the Universe when you buy that ticket that you are not going to be a burden on society to the best of your ability.

**Left, Brian is a mighty fine pal for a grand ole time at the Gentilly Stage for the Jazz & Heritage Festival in New Orleans, LA**

Look, we've all been there, when we've needed help, trust us. We have definitely benefited from the loving support of our festy ***framily***, and we have provided in return. So, don't get us wrong. It's just extremely important to underscore the importance of taking care of yourself. (We talk Health & Hygiene in the next chapter).

It's great to have tons of fun, but not at the expense of yourself. And we've seen it a lot. We love all our beautiful friends (like you, dear reader!) and want everyone who buys a ticket to a music festival to get it together, baby. This is why we present:

## PLANNING FOR HIPPIES

OK, let's back up to the elated feeling of seeing an announcement of a music festival with a great headliner and, like, two of your FAVORITE new bands and a bunch of bands you've never heard of. It's super exciting. If the stars align (See glossary: ***festy constellation***), you are going to one of those a-mazing, OMG weekends of your life.

Music festivals can be life-changing. What other events change your life? Babies, graduations, moving to new cities, right? And here's the thing: When big, amazing events occur in life, chances are you've been doing a lot of planning to make it happen smoothly.

The problem is, a lot of hippies never plan for much of anything. In order to maximize your fun, you have to be a ***long-term thinker***. It's not a matter of extra work, unless you make it so.

Certain parents of certain writing team members had friends who liked to "pre-plan" vacations. They made spreadsheets for all the clothing and equipment they may possibly need for their time away. It was a little much. But early in your festing days, this isn't a bad idea. Instead of using computer spreadsheets, use scraps of paper to write lists and lists! Like:

- Camping equipment (We'll talk about what to pack soon.)
- Foodstuffs (Figure out all the ingredients for completely planned out daily menus, including the packed meal for travel days. Keep reading, details on foodstuffs is coming too.) For the serious OCD, consider breaking down food lists into three categories:
    - food needed to purchased
    - food items that are already in the refrigerator
    - food to be prepared

The goal is to have everything that you could need and eat everything you bring – no leftovers.

Next, you must open up your closet and plan out fun outfits. The best psychedelic outfits include numerous layers, fresh every day, based on the weather forecast and music schedule, which of course you must dutifully ***print out a copy*** well in advance.

Pre-planning can work. By planning like this, you think out all your logistics well in advance, and the foggy pack-out is much easier.

Just one problem: The whole point of going to a festival is to relax and have fun. Pre-planning and planning is WORK, and, to such an extreme, unnecessary.

One year, we weren't sure we were going to be able to make our favorite music festival, Wanee, being strapped for cash. At the last minute, our wonderful friend Greg, may his generous soul rest in peace, underwrote half of our ticket. Our friend and future roommate Dave also helped make this happen. We met in a crowd while dancing to The Dead (turns out we lived in the same town, five hours away from the festival), and he happened to have one for sale at the cheaper "artist" rate. It takes a village, people. So, suddenly we were able to afford the festival, and we only had a day to throw a bunch of clothes and food in the car and go. Guess what? ***Operation Big Fun*** a big success!

In order to have a blast without much planning, you have to master the concept of self-sufficiency while at a music festival. That's an extremely important point when it comes to festival logic: <u>You must be able to fend for yourself</u>.

What does that mean, exactly? It really depends on the set-up of the festival, and figuring this part out in advance will really help you get prepared. Will you be able to park your car directly next to your campsite, or will festival organizers expect you to haul all your stuff on your back for a mile? There is <u>always</u> the chance that you'll have to haul your stuff.

One year at Farm to Family, which was a festival where normally folks could drive right in, it rained so badly in the days before the fest that the entire site was a mud pit. So, music fans pulled in with their cars packed to the gills, only to learn that they would have to haul their stuff from a far-away parking lot.

At the Lock'n festival one year, we caught a ride from Florida to Virginia with people we didn't know very well. The word was they had an RV, and we would be riding in style. My acquaintance had a teepee, so he asked us to bring Mexican blankets with the plans of everyone bedding down on top. So we packed appropriately, with crafts for the ride, a huge pile of Mexican blankets, a bicycle (that was an extremely good move, by the way – more on this in *Chapter 6: What to Bring and What Not*) and a big backpack.

Alas, first, these people pulled up to the house with a small, teardrop-shaped pull-behind trailer and a pick-up truck. As they were throwing our stuff in the back, it was clear we overdid it. But then, on the last day of the festival, they pronounced that they were going to "beat the traffic" and leave before the Allman Brothers show, which happened to be the last Allman Brothers show at a festival EVER. It would be the last time we would see one of our favorite bands that we'd enjoyed literally scores of times. No way would we miss their final show, which, by the way, we friggin paid for, m'kay?

**Right, do it the space alien girl's way and no one will get a laser beam fired at their heads. At Orange Blossom Jamboree in Brooksville, FL.**

We had to figure out another way to get back home, along with our stuff. ***The universe provides***! Our friends were happy to help, and yet their camp was well on the other side of the festival grounds. Learn from our schlep! You can always pack lighter.

It's a balancing act. You need to be able to sleep comfortably and dress appropriately, but you don't want to overdo it.

Be prepared for all types of weather. One year at the three-day Langerado festival in the Everglades, it was really hot, then it rained really hard, then it got really windy and then it got really cold. At the Gathering of the Vibes one year, it was so hot in the summer that many a hippie never thought to bring a pair of socks – until a front moved through and it was suddenly in the 50s and soggy. Thankfully, there was one vendor selling groovy, tie-dyed socks to save our chilly feet! *(Edit: Rosy's tie-dyed socked are the best.)*

You'll want to have good bedding, of course, and the best camps are a lot more than just a trusty, comfy tent. (We'll get into this later in the manual.) Pack too much, though, and your camp name might as well be what our rad friend Julie calls ***Camp Where's My ...?*** because everyone spends the whole time, foggy from late nights, hunched over bins and bags, searching for a bag of coffee or that pair of groovy tie-dyed socks. You know you brought it, because you brought everything!

Self-sufficiency at a music festival, then, includes having what you need (and ONLY what you need) to take care of yourself in terms of clothing, food and rest.

Sleep is vital. Make sure you get adequate sleep. We cannot stress this enough: Bring ear plugs and an eye mask! These items cannot be forgotten.

If you don't lay down for at least a few hours of rest, no matter how much fun you fear you'll be missing (See ***FOMO***), you're never going to last the entire festival. But, shockingly, not everyone will take our advice. Some of your festy neighbors will be up partying throughout the night. Why spend energy being annoyed by their laughter while you're trying to sleep? Simply insert your ear plugs, slip on an eye mask, and smile as your body and mind drifts to sleep.

**Left, even Bob Weir of the Grateful Dead isn't scared to miss out on a few concerts. At Lock'n Festival. Note the trusty watch and the ring, which is a compass.**

But perhaps the most important thing you need for self-sufficiency is the right attitude. The festival weekend's mission is ***Operation Big Fun***. In order to receive the love, laughter and friendship that make music festivals so special, you have to give, too. Everything you pack and everything you bring should be to fulfill the mission of producing as many smiles as your face allows.

This reminds me of a different guide that will certainly get a lot more press than this one, because, well, we aren't enlisting the help of a pricey agent (*Edit: We are open to partnerships.)* But you know – that one that says you need to look at an item in your house and ask yourself if it "brings you joy"? Yeah, packing for a music festival is a little like that.

Being prepared and self-sufficient provides the mental space you need to relax and enjoy yourself, instead of worrying about stuff. Some people tend to worry for the sake of worrying. Don't be one of those people.

This manual will break down the concept of self-sufficiency in detail, fear not. It's very much like the process of buying that ticket: Just like you have to be the one to get yourself through the ticket gate, you have to care for yourself once you're in there. But how? That's where our years of experience can help. You'd be surprised how many beautiful folks aren't maximizing this idea in a way to increase enjoyment of life.

Also, we may be jumping ahead here, but don't be one of those people who leave all their trash behind. ***Leave no trace.*** That's the epitome of self-sufficiency: You take care of yourself the entire festival, and then you leave your site in the same or better condition from how you found it. You help the festival organizers by reducing the cleanup, making another festival more likely. Plus, you can help others and make friends as a result. It's good karma.

# Chapter 2: Hygiene and Health

Are you committed to the concept of self-sufficiency and are totally stoked for your weekend? You want to do it right? Are you starting to get an idea of how much extreme fun can be had at a reasonable cost to help expand the number of hugs you get? (*Edit: We are presuming you know that science has proven how hugs help improve mental health and all kinds of other things. So come on in, come on you! Mmmmmmmm!)*

Yeah, so ... hugs. Your hygiene really ought to be on point, because there are a lot of hugs to go around during a music festival. We remember after a Dead show in Charlotte, North Carolina, finding ourselves chatting it up with a random person on a street corner as the concert let out. Suddenly, we had a very sober realization that we were simply talking to a homeless guy who lived on that street corner and probably hasn't had the luxury of a shower in quite some time. Hippie or homeless? It's a fine line!

The difference has little to do with the prevalence of deodorant.

**Left, Amanda being the amazingly sweet and wonderful person she is. Jazz Fest, New Orleans, Louisiana**

******Golden Rule of Fest Health***: <u>Don't put your hands in your mouth! You don't know where they've been.</u>

Seriously, if there's one rule about hygiene and health that a weird, singular group of first-person-plural point-of-view non-doctors can impart to any festival fan, it's that: Do not put your fingers in your mouth. Or your eyes. Or anywhere on your face. Take care with this, and you will reduce your chance of illness significantly.

This is much harder than it seems. Lots of people touch their face and mouths all the time, especially when they are camping and eating around a fire. It's OK. We're not trying to be all judge-y. Like, what are you supposed to do if your eye itches? What if something gets caught in your teeth? Ya GOTTA get that booger, *riiiight*? We get it (*Edit: sometimes*). But use a tissue or paper towel. Mind the Golden Rule, and you'll be a step ahead health-wise of the rest of your friends.

Investing in some hand sanitizer is also a good idea, but don't fall down the OCD black hole. We do not recommend getting a little squirt bottle and clipping it to the outside of your bag. That's so "Mom"! (*Edit: We love you, Mom!*)

See, regardless of how self-sufficient you are – and we've been in camps that included hot showers and private Port-O-Johns – there's a high likelihood that you will get sick as a result of your crazy-fun, running-around and drinking-Fireball-late-at-night weekend.

The post-festival, nasty sickness is referred to as the "***wook flu***," named after ***wookies***, you know those hairy creatures from Star Wars? Chewey is a wookie, we believe. That's what those ***heads*** who have dirty dreadlocks, short pants (or are those shorts long?), skate shoes and an arm-full of festival wristbands. (More on this interesting sub-culture of the brotherhood in *Chapter 4: Finding a Friend in Everyone*). The point is that wookies don't always tend to take care of themselves, and they have may have germs you don't!

Thus, hygiene is important, but challenging too, since most festivals do not offer running water. To get clean, the first thing to do is what is known as a ***hippie shower.*** (We'll break this down soon.)

Besides being all germ-scared, why worry about a couple of days without cleaning? Two words: ***festival feet***.

***Festival feet*** are legendary, notorious, infamous and just straight up disgusting. We've had 'em, and we've seen 'em up close and personal. We've smelled 'em, too. Remember, there are some things you cannot unsmell.

**Right, Nada helps repair a heady hairwrap, which involves taking colorful string and wrapping a small lock of hair permanently. We recommend trading energy work or other barter for this groovy souvenir.**

For reals, your feet are going be awfully dirty. If you are rocking flip-flops or rugged sandals like

Tevas, Keens or amazing ***rope sandals*** that we sold you, the dusty ground on which you are trudging will sink deeply into your toes and crackly, ***gnarsty*** feet. Do not, we repeat, do not get a pedicure BEFORE the festival. That is a righteous after-fest activity, however. (*Edit: Tip well, for the love of all things holy.)*

Besides your feet, you're going to want to freshen up during a festival. All that dancing and laughing and running around and acting like a kid may just remind you how old you actually are. Take our hard-fought wisdom here and look as fresh as possible. Give yourself a little time to get yourself together each day before heading to the music so you can keep being awesome.

## SHOWERING FOR HIPPIES (AKA THE FRESH SESH):

***Hippie bathday**! Enjoy it, as it only comes once a year.*

Let me come clean here (see what we did there?). We actually kinda like that body odor smell. We think it is a happy, smell-based musky memory trigger to the ***Dead lot***. Sometimes it's stinky but really there's a part of us – deep inside – that likes it. Every once in a while, though, we'll put our arm up comfortably on the back of a chair or bench and get a whiff of ourselves. And whew! *No bueno*.

The reality is that just because you are a beautiful soul reading (or writing) this manual doesn't give you an excuse to smell. Packing what you need for a hippie shower is easy. Bring your bathroom stuff in a medium-sized cloth tote bag, preferably with a logo of, say, a public radio station or something groovy on the side. Ours was a bag that was packed with dried beans, a dried herbal mixture and a ladle or something that our sister-in-law gave us that read something like, "Women's Soup Project." WTF? Anyway, extra points if your bag is a little glittery. But make sure the bag is big enough to throw in a change of clothes and a towel, but not too big that you look like a prima donna. It's nice having handles long enough to hang it on a branch or a hook. You will likely not be able find a place free of funk or wash-water runoff to put it down. Inside the bag, be sure to have travel-sized bottles of the following:

- Dr. Broenner's Magic Soap (*Edit: OMG DO NOT GET THE PEPPERMINT IN YOUR EYE*) or equivalent natural soap that makes you happy ... does this soap bring you joy? (*Edit: Insert eyeroll*)
- Shampoo and conditioner, for venues with running water
- Wet Wipes and anti-bacterial hand gel, for venues that exist in the cruel, often gross world of Port-O-Johns only
- Deodorant

- A brush or comb, if you've got hair on your head
- A toothbrush and natural toothpaste
- Lip balm and facial sunscreen with a high SPF
- An emery board
- A big safety pin
- Patchouli or other groovy scent

If you have access to running water, which can be rare, then by all means use soap on your hair and body (*Edit: Focus on the privates, honey!*). Wash under your nails while remembering the Golden Rule. Oh, geez. You already forgot the ***Golden Rule of Festival Health*** already didn't you. (*Edit: Short term memory loss is real, people!)*

We know we've been conditioning you to read the glossary (*Edit: Insert another eyeroll*) but this is worth repeating: Do not put your hands in your mouth! After a shower at a festival, you'll be all nice and tingly fresh and oh-so-clean, feeling like a million bucks! Then you won't feel the need to anxiously clean your nails with other nails and your teeth, or bite off small bits of cuticles ... oh, is this just us? We're working on it!

Showering options vary ***grately*** at festivals. Some have showers (either at a cost or for free), while others have a basic and rather depressing line of Port-O-Johns. If you are camping somewhere with a water spigot in a reasonable proximity to camp, it's a righteous idea to bring a <u>solar shower</u>. Delegate this task to one of those Boy Scout-style members of your crew, who will likely be really excited to rig it up. In fact, a good way to identify a good festy camp site is based on the proximity to running water and trees you can use to string up a few tapestries with clothes pins and some rope to create a makeshift private shower. Everyone will be so jelly!

But if no flowing water showers are available, are cost-prohibitive or are definitively a "pain in your ass" for one reason or another, a ***hippie shower*** is the way to go. There is a science to the hippie shower:

<u>Step 1: Wet Wipe(s).</u> The order of wiping is such:

1. Face
2. Privates
3. Fold and clean arm pits
4. Feet. Oh, God those feet.

This usually requires a number of wet wipes, well worth the environmental impact when you think of your impact on the universe with the number of hugs you're going to give during the day and how dirty you are.

<u>Step 2: Brush your hair</u>. If you have long hair like we have been known to have, brush hair in the evening too, if you can manage. Unless you are actively pursuing dreadlocks, prevent them. It's ***doing your future self a favor***.

Step 3: Smell better. Apply deodorant and rub on a little patchouli. This is actually doing everyone else a favor!

Step 4: Brush your teeth. (extra credit if you floss!)

Step 5: Change your clothes and *voila*! Good as new.

An important part of feeling great after that five-step ***Fresh Sesh*** is getting adequate sleep the previous night. You already have an eye mask and ear plugs on lock, but it's worth mentioning rest again. Besides looking better, you won't pass out prematurely.

This whole daily festival process is important for both men and women. Festivals strip away your everyday routine, that's for sure. Don't let it mess with your health and hygiene.

If you're a lady reading this, you may notice that make up is not part of the hippie shower. Some women feel that they must wear makeup in order to look "OK," but not as a festival. You really don't. We all love you, naked eyes and all.

Guys never wear makeup, unless, you know, they do. But, hey guys? Honest truth here: There are a lot of you who allow yourselves to look like ass with big ol' eye bags and dark circles. Not necessary. Putting in a little effort each day will help you party on and look sparkly good doing it. A visit to the Spit-

Shine Shack is just as important as knowing when to call it a night (hint: ***first light early birds***).

Our groovy friend Elizabeth plays the upright bass, and she and many of our friends enjoy picking and grinning around the campfire at Magnolia festivals late into the night. One night, we remember finally lying down around 4 a.m. while everyone was still hooting and hollering. Thank goodness for those ear plugs! As we drifted off to sleep, all we could hear was Elizabeth's faint, rhythmic bluegrass *bum-bum-bum-bum*. We smiled ourselves right to sleep.

Without minimal rest, you're likely going to first get ***grugly***, then sick. Music festivals are hard on the body, no matter how fit you are. And let's face it, most of us are the weekend warrior type anyway. If your day is mostly sitting at a desk for work, you're likely going to be pretty beat by all the walking and dancing. If you're like most festival-goers, you'll also be drinking beers and perhaps partaking in other intoxicants, which may be fun but are certainly not the healthiest, all medicinal marijuana arguments aside. The bottom line is there's a lot of stimulation; you're going to get exhausted. Take time to rest and care for yourself so you can keep going strong throughout the weekend.

**Left, Jason, Reed, Kimbo, Gwen, Chris, Danny and Tone all deserve shout-outs for being part of the writing team, even though they didn't realize it at the time and no you're not getting any royalties and we know you can't believe you actually had to buy a copy and ... guys, guys?**

## GOING TO YOUR HAPPY PLACE: A PORT-O-JOHN ACTION PLAN

If everything is going well on the inside, you'll need to go to the bathroom. Usually this is of paramount importance not long after your first cup of strong, camp coffee. Some festival facilities have bathhouses with showers, but others are strictly Port-O-John central. You need to approach these with a game plan.

In general, this classy writing team tries to lead a Port-O-John-free existence, but that can be impossible. For the uninitiated, let us explain why we try to avoid Port-O-Johns. Simply, at camping music festivals packed with people, many aren't following the care-filled advice of this Fest Life Guide! They aren't interested in self-sufficiency or taking care of themselves at all. They eat like shit and well ... the toilets can get pretty damn disgusting.

To add insult to injury, you may have to stand in line to go in one!

OK, it's ***go time.*** Check your watch. Let's make this whole thing fast. As you approach the Port-O-Johns, keep your eyes peeled for the fastest-moving line. Guys tend to let all the girls go in front of them, so pick a line that is mostly female. You may think that the "ladies room" has the long line so you should get behind the dudes, but when there are unisex Port-O-Johns, the female lines go faster. That's our proven hypothesis, anyway.

Be prepared to jump in front of someone who hesitates. People space out. You must have a laser-like focus at all times. The rule here, as always, is ***You snooze you lose.*** Hello? Haven't you been to third grade? (*Edit: See ya, sucka!*)

Keep a vigilant watch on the little color-coded locks. Is it green? It may be empty, and you're just a fool waiting there. Take EXTREME CAUTION when opening Port-O-Johns. When we try a door, we open it slowly and avert our eyes as we open it until we are completely, 100% sure it is empty. Remember, there are some things you can never unsee.

Sometimes the Port-O-John is (relatively) awesome and you've approached a freshly cleaned and provisioned potty row, but that's rare. Some key game plan points:

- Be prepared: Carry a little wad of toilet paper and, if so desired, wet wipes.
- Keep expectations low.
- Touch as few places as humanly possible.
- Squat – ALWAYS
- Advert eyes and ***Go to your happy place***.
- Do not focus on the uncouth nature of the situation or spend any mental energy on anything other than relieving yourself.
- Get in-and-out as quickly as possible.

This advice is also good for any bathroom experience at a festival. Also, do not look at yourself in the mirror. Wash your hands with lots of soap if possible. Do not linger! If you find your mind wandering, sing to yourself the classic Cypress Hill refrain: "I ain't goin' out like that, ain't goin' OUT!" (Two points if we just gave you an earworm.)

If, perchance, you're camping with a large group of friends, consider pitching in together and getting a private Port-O-John. You can lock it. One rad crew we've camped with connects a bright orange cone to the key and hangs it in a central location that only we know about. (*EDIT: Our friends are pissed now. Guys, seriously – no one is going to find it after reading this! We can barely find it! Besides, is anyone reading this?)*

**Right, to make our friends like us again, here is a picture of Kofi Burbridge, keyboardist and flutist of the Tedeschi Trucks Band at the Sunshine Music Festival in Boca Raton, FL. Note the rad Third-Eye Pine necklace. Thank you Harvey! We still love this gift!**

We like to string some battery-powered lights inside the private potty and clean up after ourselves. It's well worth the $5-10 per person. The rental company will clean it out every day, and drunks stumbling by will express their jealousy. That's self-sufficiency to the extreme.

Hygiene is very important for having fun at a music festival, and health is crucial too. You need to drink plenty of water and eat right, too. Bring chewable vitamin C tablets and pop at least 1,500 milligrams throughout the day. Really! You'll be around a lot of people who smoke, and maybe you smoke. Hey, I'm not judging ... although really, we love you! Don't kill yourself with cigarettes! Come on! We need you. Did you know smoking depletes vitamin C? And vitamin C is nature's antibiotic, so eat up. It goes a long way to keeping you healthy.

Water is also of utmost importance. One year at a Wanee festival, one member of this writing crew (who has gone through a depressing number of failed relationships) and her then-boyfriend had finished up the gallons of spring water we had brought along. When we tried to get some water from a nearby spigot, it was so cloudy and sulfuric that it was undrinkable. There was no more water for sale at the nearby store. If it wasn't for a kindly neighbor, we might have had to leave early or, worse, go to Wal-Mart in the middle of the festival. Sometimes neighbors do (mostly beer) runs, and to those people, we salute you.

One last note under health and hygiene chapter: Adequate nutrition is really important. You can bring all your vitamins and mineral supplements but come on. It's vacation. You're probably stoked to eat junk all weekend. But don't do it. There's a whole chapter on this: *Chapter 5 Foodstuffs = Fuel*. But before we get to this, let's talk about what's really important at a music festival. Music!

# Chapter 3:
# Music as a Priority

We know, up to now, the ***newbs*** might be worried about why the hell they are putting themselves through all the risks to their health and leaving the comforts of ***couch-tour.*** For those who aren't in the know, "couch tour" is a wonderful alternative to actually going to a music festival, if you really, really can't go. The three-prong test of date-line-up-location often fails at one or more prong. Couch tour is one answer to ***FOMO***. Many festivals offer live video streams of certain stages, so you can jam out at home without, you know, not wearing pants.

But it's simply not the same. Music festivals provide meaningful opportunities to feel, react and interpret the energies that surround and originate from the creation of live music. Community is paramount, but music is the priority! With all the distractions and fun of festivals, this is an easy thing to forget. We're all here for the music.

We are partial to running with our friend Adam at festivals. Adam is a videographer who has an impressive collection of live music shown on his YouTube channel, Cheeseheadmusic. (What up, Adam!) We remember SunFest one year in West Palm Beach, the line up was really great: The Wailers, Inner Circle, Blues Traveler and Michael Franti all in one day! The problem was, their sets overlapped and the stages on which these great artists were playing were located on the way other side of the festival grounds. Adam prioritizes music, and so do we. We booked it back-and-forth to the different festival stages that day and, as a result, saw a bunch of great music and had a blast.

Look, there are a lot of ***yucks*** at festivals, lots of slaps on the backs and goofing off.

We love laughing, of course, but all in good time. If done at an inappropriate time, it can quickly turn into what is known in some circles as ***donkey dicking***. (This phrase is most appropriately used in relation to a Gov't Mule-inspired rage stick. Now that's an ass sticking we can get behind!) It's great to crack jokes and all, but you are at the festival to see live music.

**Left, the queen of yucks and her royal highness, Doug and Jen, ladies and gents. These two? Serious music lovers. No, no, we're serious! Yuck yuck yuck.**

Remember that expensive ticket you purchased? You didn't buy it to just hang out with the people you could see at a bar anytime. It's to experience live music performance and creative experience that can rejuvenate and transform you. ***"There's live music happening!"*** is a phrase you'll hear us say with frequency. So easy we forget.

Music is powerful, and if you don't know it – then go see more live music! We remember seeing a Sunday morning "gospel" set at Magnolia Festival by The Lee Boys. This entire writing team grew up Catholic, but dropped out of that club. Gospel isn't exactly our favorite genre. But The Lee Boys have a song called "Miss You" and we'll tell you what: We felt it. They channeled our grandmother, who had died a few months prior. And we did miss her and hadn't fully mourned her. Tears streamed down our collective face as we sang along. It was such a positive and loving song. It felt wonderful to connect and sing love surrounded by friends. We've also shed some nice tears to "I Can't Make You Love Me" sung live by Bonnie Raitt and J.J. Grey & Mofro's "The Sun Is Shining Down," to name a few more.

There are endless examples of music's power to heal and bring joy: Hula-hooping in a flow to Rusted Root's "Food and Creative Love." Skipping across a field to Railroad Earth's "Smiling Like a Buddha." Dressed up in a Toto costume (more on this in *Chapter 7: Making it Happen*) and ***riding the rail*** while Dumpstaphunk performed a Parliament Funkadelic Halloween show. Music can be so life affirming!

This is why ***"There's live music happening!"*** is one of our mantras. This is to be said aloud at the campsite, if one discovers being dragged into the giggles with friends who, understandably, are enjoying each other's company during a music festival. We get it. It's a balance. But you can (and should) hang out with those goofballs after the music is over. Right then and only right then, there's a performance that will never happen again. Prioritize!

Be in the know about what band is playing when and where. This is not as easy as it seems. There is a three-part process here. First, you need to know who. Then you need to know when. And then you need to know where. Let's break these down:

**Above, Applebutter Express at Hulaween in Live Oak, FL. What Up Hometeam!**

The Who: (We saw them play for free ... a mix of meh and bucket listing if there ever was one.) ***Print a copy*** of the schedule before you leave. ALSO! When you arrive, be sure to grab the smallest version/easiest to understand schedule of any printed booklet that may come to you at the gates. Have both, and have them handy. Bare necessities to have with you at all time: The music schedule, one paper towel, lip balm, a lighter and possibly 50 glow sticks. But more on this soon.

The When: Sure, the schedule tells you your favorite band plays at 7 p.m. But what the heck is the time? Be a helpful, prepared person and ***wear a watch.*** It is the missing piece of the getting-your-act-together puzzle that so many people forget. We know you want to be all *Easy Rider* and throw your watch on the ground before the festival, but save the drama for Henry Fonda. You need that watch.

The Where: Remember Adam scrambling back and forth to see reggae at SunFest? It's vital to know where the stages are. The more you know ... (*Edit: We just dated ourselves, didn't we.)*

The reality is that, no matter how prepared you are, no matter how many times you've obsessively scanned the schedule in happy anticipation of high-quality live music, you will endlessly be looking at your watch and then looking at the schedule and then looking back at your watch. And repeat. It's amazing how your head becomes a hole-y sieve after a day at a music festival. Seriously. Who is playing at noon on which stage?

The best festivals have the best schedules, but usually there are very hard choices that must be made. ***You can't do everything.***

Sometimes the organizers are real jerks, overlapping fabulous acts. Other times, you may have to choose between a band you know and love and one that you've been meaning to check out. Not sure who to check out? Poll the audience!

Your friends, new and old, will have much to say about the bands, if they have their priorities right. Listen so you can discover something new.

**Left, good people including Julie, Philip, Kassidy and Duncan, who had a good remedy when we got poison ivy after festival camping. Don't worry – the rash only showed up where clothes didn't cover. We rocked scarves Stevie Nicks-style for a good 10 days.**

That's really one of our very favorite parts of going to music festivals: the ***festival find.*** (This is different than a ***ground score,*** explained in the next chapter.) What band have you never listened to and will suddenly simply connect with? Our lives are so much richer, thanks to all the new music that we otherwise would have never come across were it not for the festival scene. Back in 1995, stumbled upon the Drive-By Truckers at Langerado Festival. Now, that band has had a lot of incarnations since then, but boy oh boy we loved 'em! Our boyfriend at the time (*Edit: Oh, he stole money from you too?*) learned "Goddamn Lonely Love" on the guitar, and we sang it together before realizing it was just the foreshadowed theme song of the relationship.

Yes, music is the priority because it can impact your life so greatly. Thus, another Golden Rule: ***The Golden Rule of Festival Crowds:*** Talkers in the back! All festivals are general admission, except for the VIP section (which is discussed in *Chapter 9: Life on the Road*). That means there are no seats and everyone is free to roam about the vicinity, which is awesome. So, if you get there before we do, or your friends do and you're able to squeeze up to enjoy the show with them, or if you just want to get up front and shimmy past us, or whatever, you're in front of us. And you know what, that's OK! We have two plans in the crowd: Either we're up close to see the musicians actually playing their instruments and interacting with each other (Every member of the writing team is petite, what.) or we will be in the back, somewhere with enough space for dancing.

Do not expect a lot of room when you're up close. You shouldn't get too knocked around, but be realistic. There's no need for elbowing and taking up more than your fair share of standing room when you are close. Relax. Don't excrete too much testosterone in the front section of the crowd (*Edit: Or anywhere, really*). Space is not something you should really expect within the first 25 yards or so of the stage at a huge venue. But what you should expect, especially if you're near the soundboard, is to be able to hear better than those behind you.

**Right, good festy buddies including Jen, Elena, Barry, Jeanne and Leo. Bad-ass tie-dye mandala dress courtesy of Bubba's Love Dyes.**

It's just plain WRONG to talk loudly when you're up close at a concert. It's rude. People are there to listen to the band, and only those on stage should be heard. The concert is not the time to talk to your friend about whether the girl likes you or discuss your favorite beer or debate what to eat for dinner. SHUT UP! (Bob Weir, the Grateful Dead vocalist/guitarist, famously said, ***"STFU!"***)

Despite our general patience and compassion for our fellow fans, we also have low tolerance for those who sing along very loudly, unless it's a situation where the lead singer of the band encourages it. J.J. Grey & Mofro have a song called "Lockloosa." It's lovely ... except when the entire drunken crowd yells the lyrics at the top of their lungs along with the band. We are not here to hear you sing. You can sing along in your head or quietly. The last time we heard J.J. perform it, he had given in to the reality that he would no longer be able to sing his song without the drunks bellowing, so he asked everyone to sing along. That's enabling, J.J.!

Same can be said for bringing instruments: Don't do it! News flash! You are not in the band! We had another boyfriend who liked to clap double-time with the band because he played the drums and could generally clap along to the beat. But he was not in the band, sorry dude. We liked to turn and insert an outstretched palm in between his clapping hands. ***#Sorrynotsorry***. He was enjoying himself, and that's important, but he was distracting from the music.

Fun is important, but music is the priority. The two shouldn't have to be mutually exclusive. In fact, we find it very fun to honor my favorite musicians with our undivided attention, wicked cool dance moves and participation when requested (*EDIT: Although, really, Michael Franti, how are we doin'? Great! We promise, we are great. Yes. We're still doin' good, thanks for asking. Jump up and down, you ask? Well, OK. Put our hands up in the air? I guess so. Are you going to play a song if we do this? YES WE JUST SAID WE WERE FINE!!)*

Enjoy the musical experience in person, because you are actually there, in the now. <u>Experience with your eyes, not your phone's camera.</u> It's not necessary and quite discouraged to hold up your device above your head and record the whole show. *Hi. It's the people behind you in the third row. We are trying to see the musician as well.* You are not a professional videographer! With the advent of YouTube, you are almost always guaranteed to find some footage after the fact. Is Jimi Hendrix lighting his guitar on fire? OK, grab a little video. But just a few minutes, max. It's simply not fair to the people behind you to pretend to be Steven Spielberg up there. Enough! Be here now! You will remember it if it's really that awesome to you, we promise.

In fact, upon entering the concert area, we believe there should be a system in which everyone must determine honestly on a scale from 1 to 10 how much they really want to be there, and this will be the means by which we determine who stands in front of whom. It's incredibly frustrating to be an "8" and know that the kids who are in front of us, chatting loudly with each other, are a "4." And yet, in the ***G.A.*** world, we have no real claim to be in front of them. (*EDIT: Until this Fest Guide, bitches!*)

That's why if you really want to see a particular band, go early. Plan it out. Don't get frustrated! Go early, grab a spot right at the front – ***riding the rail*** means you can lean up against the steel barrier that keeps us crazed and drugged-out fans from the hard-working musicians. It's a most sought-after spot because it's comfortable (unless there are Hell's Angels around, but we don't think that really happens anymore) and there is no one blocking your view. No one talking loudly, no one really distracting you. Folks who have these primo spots are either quick movers (always keep your eyes open for people getting ready to leave the rail and move fast) or arrive early. Go prepared with water and perhaps a beer, and take a seat before the show starts. Stake your claim but don't be a jerk about it.

So, OK, test time! (*EDIT: AWW MAN!*) Here's a little scenario for you: You've done everything right up to now. You're cool. You come early and get a good spot. It's not the rail but it's close enough. You're really happy and ready. You've got a beverage. Life is good. And then suddenly some kid who is pals with the kid in front you crams in, because little did you know that the person in front of you was holding a place for some jerk who is smoking right in your face, recording everything with his device and talking endlessly. What do you do?

<u>Option 1:</u> Tell the kid to get it under control in the coolest way possible. Say something like: "Hey, would you mind not talking so much? Also, your cigarette is kinda right in my face. See this burn mark?" (*EDIT: Maybe buy extra copies of this guide for situations such as this?* ***Just sayin'****!)*

<u>Option 2:</u> Get in a fight. This is not cool. That kid needs to get out of your space that you claimed way before he came around. What is his problem, anyway? He's obviously a newb, and you're friggin'

sick of these stupid kids coming in and crapping on your GOOD TIME!

Option 3: Move.

Option 1 is a great first step, but it rarely works. Not everyone is fully aware of the importance of caring and supporting others. A lot of people are really self-absorbed. (*EDIT: Sorry to break the news.*)

Option 2 seems natural. Some people get really territorial because they put effort to following the code of behavior and the Golden Rule for being in a crowd and someone else has a better spot and is ruining it for you. It is not fair, and it sucks. We all agree with you. Here, let us hug you. Luckily, there is a benefit to general admission. You can move. So, move. It's OK. You can't change other people; you can only change yourself. Just move and enjoy the show.

It took us a little while to really understand the power of just moving a few feet or so to the left or right. And we have a little story from our very first festival to explain this:

Wanee #1! We found ourselves in the second row at the Allmans Brothers show. They were the headliners, and everyone was stoked. We arrived early with our friends in the hope of front row, but when we arrived there was a row of (empty) camping chairs already set up in front of us. So, we sat down and waited for the music to begin. It ended up being a family consisting of a mom and dad, plus a little kid or two. It was late and everyone was partying; festivals aren't really a place for kids, often, but whatever. The mom was in front of me, and the kids were a few spots over, sitting bored in their front row seats. We didn't care too much about this, except for the fact that they had given themselves way too much room on the rail for a crowd of thousands. The only reason two more people weren't up there? Their stupid chair barricade.

The show began and the Brothers were killing it, but the security guard was real upset because there were a few people behind us videotaping the show. We guess that was a no-no. The guards kept jumping over the barrier, pushing through the camping chairs and putting their hands up to cover the cameras behind us. This happened a few times ***because, hippies.***

The fourth time or so, we took a chance and follow the security guard through the family's chair blockade and made a move for the rail next to the mom. She – who, it turns out, had a manicure and was dressed head-to-toe in a matching orange and blue University of Florida Gators attire, complete with coiffed hair piled artfully under a visor – puts her hands on both our shoulders and literally pushes us back, yelling, "Oh no you don't!"

**Right, speaking of hippies, Chris and Teresa at Magnolia Festival in Live Oak, FL – near the very spot where this story takes place!**

Whoa.

OK! Quiz time! (*EDIT: AGAIN!?*)

Does she have the right to save extra space in a crowd by blocking access because she arrived with her chair before us? Should she have put her hands on us? Discuss amongst yourself. What would you do here?

Here's what happened: We looked down at the remaining two-ounce dredges of dark beer that a friend had given us that we were drinking but didn't really like because it was too hoppy, and *oops*! Oh our gosh! It spilled out of the cup all down her fancy outfit! Oh no! Did someone push us from behind? Oh whoopsie doodles!

In slow motion, suddenly, consequences appeared. Her tall and redneck-y husband was hovering over our doe-eyed selves, who were mentally preparing ourselves to get punched in the collective face. Immediately, a security guard appears and waves his finger at us, ordering us to exit the crowd by climbing over the front row barrier. We try to protest but there was no way around it. We were being ejected. But it was actually kind of awesome, because suddenly we were BEYOND THE RAIL! We were really up close! *Go Gregg Allman! Warrrrrrrennnnnn Haynes! Wooooo! Derek Trucks you are slaaaaaaying it!*

We'll tell you the rest of the story now, but from here it veers away from the moral of the story, which is ***don't be a jerk*** in the crowd.

The guard ushered us to the side and told us to wait. Then this random hippie guy, who we did not know, appeared and decided to plea our case to the security guard: "Aw, come on, man! Let her go, man!" The guard ignored him until he does a distraction crime! He ran in a very large circle in a strangely menacing way, and the guard falls for it! He chases after the kid and leaves my side!

Quiz time again! Would you run?

Here's what happened: We didn't run. We stayed put, because what the hell was actually going on here? We don't own a television, and this whole situation was hilarious! The guard comes back, because of course he gets the kid, and the three of us head back to ... *wait for it* ... behind the stage! Sweet!

**Left, we interrupt this great story to bring you these lovely ladies including Dana, Lauren, Jessica and Jan.**

OK, backstage is awesome! It's a big, outdoor area with a bunch of trailers and the steps up to the stage. We ask slyly to go to the bathroom while motioning politely toward a trailer, but the guard immediately sees through that. Oh well ... there's Gregg on stage! Butchie! So fun! We wait for a short bit, and then the guard's boss emerged at the stage door. The kid started off, "Hey man, come on, we didn't do anything wrong and ..."

Big Boss Man cut him off: "SHUT UP OR I'LL PUT A 12 IN YOUR MOUTH!"

Whoa.

It's about that time when the boss realized, indeed, we are totally not a problem. Conveniently, we were not really drunk or anything because we had spent so much time staking out our killer second-row spot. He made us promise never to go near that woman again, which we really wouldn't want to anyway, nor would it really be even possible to snake through the thousands of people in the crowd to return to that spot, and off we went.

Another quiz question: Do you put any energy toward saving the random hippie kid who tried to be your unrequested advocate?

Now don't be ridiculous! We let him fend for himself, hoping that he would never have a "12 in his mouth." Five minutes later, we were enjoying a fresh beer in our hand and skipped off to enjoy the rest of the music. That's right, music first!

(As an prologue to the story, our buddy Danny had witnessed us getting ushered from our spot and "taken out back." While we were gallivanting around, he arrived back to camp to inform our whole crew that we'd been kicked out of the park and was likely already in shackles and an orange jumpsuit. We soon returned to victoriously proclaim, ***"The man can't keep me down!"***)

Fast forward a decade plus, and we have a very different perspective. Could I have gotten up to the front row with honey instead of vinegar, you know, like attracting bees? Maybe not, but we would have had a better chance. (*EDIT: We were a little jerky, now weren't we.*) That's why it's important to find a friend in everyone, even the bitchy Gators fan. This lesson gets its own chapter (*4*). But it's also extremely important, when finding friends, to stay safe.

# Chapter 3a.: Safety Third

Haha! We love that saying: Safety Third! Its origin is in the fire-spinning community, who, think about first the safety of the audience, then the safety of the venue, then safety of self. By the way, we also love those who flow with fire! Our friends who spin in the Treasure Coast Fire Troupe were featured performers at Hulaween a couple years ago, and they spun fire poi, a staff and a hoop. (For more, see *Chapter 8: Making it Happen*). They were awesome, even though JT got a nasty burn on his shoulder. But he kept on performing and smiling because Safety Third!

Of course, this tongue-in-cheek saying can also be used for all attendees of music festivals. If music is the priority, then fun is number two and safety is a straight-up third. (*Edit: It's true, Mom! Yeeeew!)*

That being said, don't be like a guy we were dating one year during an Orange Blossom Jamboree music festival in Florida: We were mere hours into the festival when he stumbled (drunkenly, if memory serves) in the dark in a field and twisted his ankle. Hobbling for the rest of the time was a bummer! There are always going to be divots and obstacles in your path. ***Constant vigilance*** – it's the only way.

**Left, the cool Brotherly Love Productions crew at Sunfest includes Pat, the Becks, Erica, the Duclos family, Chris, Eric and many more.**

Look around you to avoid pitfalls. Be aware of your surroundings. Looking on the ground when you're walking is actually good practice for another reason: ***ground scores***!

This has nothing to do with safety but it's a wonderful reality of music festivals. People leave stuff behind all the time! By simply looking on the ground, we've found: a headlamp, a handy steel cup with a carabineer, a pretty sarong, a Grateful Dead-themed handkerchief, money, a 3D poster, a stadium blanket, one of those plastic hand clappers, an Uno card that someone interestingly taped a space scene on the playing side, plus all kinds of other things that have come and go. When the concert is over and people pack up their stuff and leave the grounds, by all means, whip out your flashlight and walk around for a couple minutes before milling out of the field. You may find something super-cool! Of course, make sure whatever you find is puke-free and isn't something someone put on their head or in their mouth. That's just nasty. Also make sure the owner is really gone. We once had a Naglene water bottle, covered with a bad ass OM sticker that we took everywhere, taken from the ground near our friend's blanket. Ya win some, ya lose some.

*(EDIT: Important: Never take any drugs that you've found on the ground, no matter how tempting that might be.)*

In fact, it's the safety chapter, so let's talk about drugs. Sit down. No, no, it's OK. This is as uncomfortable for me as it is for you. Now, have you done the drugs? Look, we're not judging you, honey. You just need to tell us the truth. Because we were in your room while you were at your crummy job at the grocery store earlier today, and, well, we looked in your bag. We found the drugs. We really can't believe you. You're not who we thought you were. Get rid of those drugs. And we mean flush it down the toilet, not take them all in an all-out rager with your friends. Now go to your room! GO! GO! *bursts into tears*

Sorry, we just had a flashback.

Drugs are a part of music festivals for many (let's face it, most) people, but not everyone. There are beautiful people known as "Wharf Rats," or the sober people at Grateful Dead shows. If you look for them at a festival, you will find group meeting to get the strength to stay sober and enjoy the festivities. They wear stickers that read, "***One Show at a Time,***" and we honor them. Do not take one of those stickers and wear it while drinking a beer; that is frowned upon.

It isn't easy to have a slightly different definition of "partying" than what feels like everyone else at the festival. One festival we attended happened to be the weekend before a big drug test for a great new job. That meant no smoking reefer. Another festival happened in the middle of Lent one year, when, even though we dropped out of the Catholic club when we were kids, we gave up alcohol for 40 days. That was interesting. Man, we have a lot of friends who only socialize with a beer in their hands. That fest, we had a couple drinks, because we were pretty sure God was cool with it, but infinitely less than we normally would have. And guess what? We still had a fantastic time.

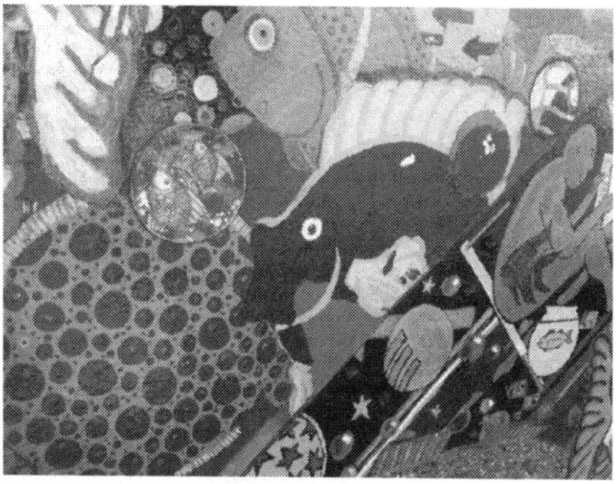

**Right, a detail of the Merry Prankster's Furthur Bus, as seen at The Gorge in George, Washington. Next the bus, some dude gave us a small piece of paper and tried to tell us it was free acid. Oh, always pranking!**

But let's just be blunt: Drugs can be fun!

Psychedelics like magic mushrooms and acid are still popular long after the '60s because, *if you have stable mental health*, they are a great way to spend between four and eight hours when you otherwise have nothing to do except make music a priority (and fun a close second!). Marijuana is legal in a bunch of places and getting more and more accepted as normal in the United States and throughout the globe each day. There are lots of other drugs on the scene, of course. We can't even begin to list them all, if for no other reason than the list will become woefully outdated by the time we are finished writing this sentence.

Here's an important point about drugs: ***You don't have to do them all.*** Make a drug plan, if you are leaning in that direction. And don't feel like you have to! Drinking a couple beers or even coconut water all weekend can be perfect. We had some amazing kombucha in a Phish lot one year! You are not cooler just because you ingest a lot of chemicals.

Our recommendation is to be smart about the drugs. Do you have a mental imbalance? BE HONEST. If you are prone to depression or split personalities, just say no. We once camped with a girl who was really nice; we even had entire conversations with her about her sister, who was getting married, and *yada yada* – UNTIL she took the mushrooms. First, she ate a pot brownie, and then she tripped. And she was never the same. Seriously, it was scary! She had a permanent look of extreme fear in her eyes at everyone, especially, it felt, us. (Turns out everyone felt uncomfortable by this rapid change.) Her kind boyfriend had to shepherd her from one place to another, ultimately leading her, we believe, to an emergency room for some chemical shot that balanced her brain out. And all's well that ends well, we guess. But she was no fun to be around. Don't do that to your camp mates.

At this point, maybe you're smiling a toothy grin in the mirror and shaking your head, confident you've got all your marbles so *no problemo*. It's not that simple with drugs. We would like to share the time when ***Operation Big Fun*** was in full effect, with Giant Panda Guerilla Dub Squad on the stage at night and we were surrounded by our pals Bradley,

Scroggie and the rest of Short Cut Camp. Short Cut brought a massive amount of neon glowing toys with them, and we were the ones with the toothy grins when we agreed to meet up at camp and ***travel like a family*** to the show. We were marching excitedly to the music with neon bop guns, glowsticks jutting out of dreadlocks and pockets, stuck inside balloons – so alight that we could have been mistaken for a psychedelic army. We were having a blast right in the front of the concert, dancing and laughing when suddenly: A woman next to us fell down in the crowd and started convulsing right at our feet. We looked down in horror as seriously, foam was coming out of her mouth in a seizure. We immediately ran through the throngs for a nearby security guard. (Running *toward* the guard – there's a first for everything.) We found one and when we returned with the guard, she was standing up again, brushing herself off and acting like nothing had happened. But it did happen, and it was scary.

If you do decide to partake in some illegal goodies, which we would never encourage in print, here are some other good tips:

Be intuitive about from whom you purchase said goodies. Drug dealers come in all shapes and sizes, and there are the good guys and the bad guys. Some are swindlers who will sell you bad drugs and take your good money. Some are friends who just want you to have the fun you want to have. Understand the difference. Just because someone wanders by your camp site offering drugs does not make the person immediately bad. But they may be – what does your gut tell you? Do not fear that you won't be able to get the high you seek, but, importantly, ***get it while the gettin's good.*** Do not be a snob. You are buying drugs, you know. All we know is that whenever we felt like the drug dealer was shady and my friends felt otherwise and bought something, we were always right. Trust yourself, since whatever results from the interaction will be your experience and your experience alone.

<u>Don't mix and match</u>. A lot of people do. Many, many of our beautiful, smart and kind friends will have a beer, then take a shot of Fireball, then smoke a joint, then eat some Cheetoes and then munch a chocolate magic mushroom. We resemble that statement. But what exactly are you experiencing? On Jam Cruise one year, our friend and we were laughing and having a glorious time, when we were offered some "Molly Magic Punch." What the hell? He took a sip, we politely declined. Understand what you're doing. Do not succumb to peer pressure. If you don't want to do something, don't. And if your friends try to make you feel bad about your decision, well, honey, they really aren't your friends.

<u>Don't overdo it</u>. Know your limits. In the mood to experiment? Do your homework first (Remember

Dan's warning in the introduction? Fellow festies provide the best wisdom.) At Hulaween, one friend gave another some acid. He wasn't used to eating acid, so he really didn't know his tolerance. We ended up separating at one point in the evening, and when we came back to the camp everyone wanted to talk to us: "How well did we know our friend, exactly?" Turns out he freaked. It was Halloween night, and my friend dressed up in a pretty awesome Thor costume. The story goes that somehow, someone was able to swindle him out of his hammer, the most important prop of the costume, and our friend was pissed! In his inebriated state, he was wandering from camp site to camp site, demanding to know who stole his hammer. We guess he thought, hey, it has to be around here somewhere! One of these 12,000 people *has* it! Of course, he never found it and, instead, made an ass out of himself.

**Left, never one to make an ass out of herself is this pretty lady, Ms. Holly, tough as nails and sweet as sorghum.**

Be smart. Cops are everywhere, and we have a story to prove it:

So, we had a big night at one of the Wanee festivals, so we were going to take it easy the following night. We were relatively sober and relaxed as we donned a simple tan, hemp tank top and dark brown pants and meandered toward the music. On our way, we saw our friend Prosperity working the Light Up Wire booth. Light Up Wire is groovy LED wire for bicycle spokes, costumes, camps and a million other great things. As we chatted, she pulled out a white belly-dancing waist wrap of glittering and clinking metal medallions and told us that we should be wearing it. She wrapped it around our waist as a gift, and we hugged her. Then we continued toward the music and saw our friend Magoo, who was working his cool tent (more on this righteous brother in *Chapter 7: The Vend Life*.) We told Magoo we were considering buying one of his mini-dresses covered with a print of the unique psychedelic artist Alex Gray's design. He was one of the few to have official license of that artist, and they were eye-catching, to say the least. He said, "I'll tell you what. If you promise to wear it now, I will give you one. Then you'll be a walking billboard for me." How could we say no? Suddenly, our look went from understated to totally insane with psychedelic art on my shirt and a glittery belt making a gentle noise with every move. Onward toward the music ... you know the priority!

In the crowd, we saw friends Megan and Andrew a few rows from the front. We hung out for a bit as the band began to play. Then we wanted to get our dance on, so we parted from our friends and decided to move back to a hill where there was more room to let loose. While dancing by ourselves in this crazy outfit, a man walked up and stood next to us, slightly uncomfortably.

We noticed him immediately. He was white, taller than 6 feet, with glasses and short, cropped hair. He was wearing a red T-shirt, jean shorts and an interesting sleeveless jean jacket. It was covered neatly with evenly spaced patches, but none had a logo I recognized. No Grateful Dead Steal Your Face,

Widespread Panic or anything. One patch was a mysterious red "A" with wings. We checked out the vest with a sideways glance. No judgment, whatever. Then we looked down: He had on clean, white Reebok sneakers. Oh geez. ***6 UP*!** (*Edit: See glossary for full translation, and if you're too lazy, let us help: COP!)*

So, hey, whatever. We were just dancing. Looking slightly ***bizarro***, of course, but we know we have the right to let our freak flag fly! We continued with our amazingly impressive dance moves, when the guy suddenly turns his body toward us. In his hand was an empty marijuana pipe and a lighter, and we stopped dancing. We looked from it to his face, which is smiling manically and nodding rapidly in an encouraging manner.

What the hell? Who offers an empty pipe to someone next to them? We presume, maybe, he wanted us to fill his pipe, smoke it and then offer it to him? Our mamas didn't raise no fools. Not going to happen.

"Hey, no thanks, brother," we said, like duh.

Immediately, his entire body crumpled into a sulk. He put the pipe in his pocket and slowly walked away. Well, we watched him: He walked to the end of the row where we were, not talking to anyone, and then walked about five rows ahead of us and moved into the crowd. He talked to no one. Then he got his phone out and seemed to have sent a text. Then he stood there for a couple minutes, and then he exited that row and walked toward the end of the field. But instead of heading out the way everyone else would go to head back to the campground, he turned to the right and ducked behind the food vendors into a black trailer that we hadn't even noticed before.

He was a cop, and he tried to set us up. Good try, fool! Ain't going out like that, AIN'T GOING OUT!

See, that's an important point when it comes to safety: You are in charge of your own safety, like, ***big picture safety.*** There are cops everywhere at music festivals, and you do not want to get yourself in jail over ***Operation Big Fun***. You have to be smart at all times. Cops may think they know better than you. Sometimes they do. When our friend's ex-boyfriend Jay stripped naked and pooped in the middle of the vending area because he was really, really high and he himself and he alone thought it was hilarious? Yeah, send that dude to the ER. Good call, coppers.

Most of the time, however, we're going to go out on a limb here and suggest that police officers do not have the same concept of fun as hippies. Case in point, you are very likely to see a ***hippie on the run*** from the cops at a music festival. In fact, think of it as a game: One point for every hippie you see running away from authority. There's nothing a good hippie – especially those of the ***wook*** variety – loves like a good outrunning of the cops. Police officers are usually older and fatter; wooks are lean, mean, running-from-cops machines. Go brother go!

Sometimes all a wook really just wants to be is a ***freaker by the speaker***, but we also wouldn't recommend this, either.

**Left, paranoia will destroy ya ... Nixon in the crowd. We said, "Hey! You're a crook!" He looked at us and replied, "I am not a crook."**

Here's something we definitely recommend: <u>Bring ear plugs to the show!</u> Remember how you packed them so that you could sleep at night and wake up feeling refreshed? Pack extra, so that you can hear that night as well. It is CRAZY how loud music festivals are. We mean, really ... we get it: PAAAARTTTAAAYY. The people in the back also need to hear. But sometimes the music is too loud, painfully loud. Oh gosh, hello Gov't Mule kick drum at Ashefest! GOT IT! WOOO! Can we turn it down a little now? To get anywhere close to the front of the stage, and certainly if you ride the rail, ear plugs are a must.

Not everyone is into ear plugs, so let's discuss this because it's actually more than just an audio safety issue. Most of your festy friends will not have ear plugs, but we are very much in favor of wearing ear plugs for many reasons. First of all, bad hearing runs in our family. (Our grandmother was known for saying, ***"What happened?"***) We also have poor olfactory glands, but that's a different story (and wonderful during those Port-O-John visits). The last thing we want to have happen is to lose our hearing permanently just because we like to have a blast at music festivals. That's just not being smart. Everyone comes back to camp after the headlining act, and they're yelling at each other. It's not because they're having such an epic time; it's for the same reason that they were yelling conversation earlier over the music. Their hearing is temporarily damaged. We're not ear doctors, but we'll play one in this Fest Life Guide.

We have another reason why ear plugs are wonderful: Because music is a priority! Ear plugs tune out all but the loudest-volume sound, which of course is the blasting music. All the chitter-chatter around us of drunks and kids who don't know any better fades away. It's easier to concentrate on the music, which is, of course, *why you are here*. It also sends a signal to the annoying people in the crowd who try to talk to us during the guitar solo or something. Ear plugs say, "Shhh!" When people talk to us, we must take out an ear plug to listen. With ear plugs, people only interrupt our enjoyment of the music for more important things: Like, "Hey, I'm going to go get a beer. Do you want anything?" We love that.

The best kind of ear plugs are the kind that are attached to a little string that loops behind your head. They aren't easy to find, so buy a bunch when you find them. Jam Cruise hooked us up with a set in a little container. Thanks Cloud 9! We bring the container with earplugs in our backpack, and when we get searched, guards always open up that little container first. When they see we are responsible and care about our hearing, they really don't look much further. ***Just sayin'.***

But just because you have ear plugs in doesn't mean that you shouldn't be looking sharp! And I'm not talking about ***festy fashions***, people (That's covered in *Chapter 6*!). Keep your eyes peeled – at the stage, of course, and also around you.

That may be the most important lesson when it comes to safety: Know what's up.

Problem is, knowing a safe scene and a safe person is truly and totally subjective. You have to trust your gut and your wisdom. Trust your smart, long-time friends who have been around the block and have always helped you in the past. Don't get paranoid! Everyone, repeat after us: ***Paranoia Will Destroy Ya!*** Instead, manifest your own success in

***Operation Big Fun*** at the music festival. If the security guard kicks you out? Manifest your own safety. Cops try to trap you in some weird drug bust? Know what's up. Running from the cops? You got it, bro. Make it happen.

# CHAPTER 4: FINDING A FRIEND IN EVERYONE

So, OK. Let's recap: Music is number one, safety is third. Number two, as you recall (Ugh, short term memory, damn you!), is fun! But what really supersedes this list is ... wait for it ... ***love***.

That's right, love is all there is! Love love love ... and now the Fest Life Guide careens down a glorious hippie hole filled with colorful flowers in a fractal design that spins away from the center of your blissed-on vision in a beautiful pattern of happiness and goodness. La la la, it goes along to the sound of music, and a big smile grows on your face as your cheeks blush and your shoulders relax! Dig it, babies, as life is so super-beautiful!

This moment of peace is brought to you by love. Love, which helps you find a friend in everyone.

Indeed, one of the most special parts of going to a music festival – and why this manual is dedicated to our ***framily*** – is to make new friends. Here's the thing: The lineup of musical acts, in many ways, narrows down the type of people who will be at the festival. Because you are also at that festival, you have things in common with the people around you. Like gangsta rap? You probably won't be at the bluegrass festival. And vice versa.

**Right, Zach Deputy, a great looper and funky multi-instrumentalist who we saw in locations throughout the globe, including here in Jupiter, Florida at Guanabana's.**

We were in Fort Lauderdale, Florida one time with a boyfriend and saw all these people in black T-shirts and stringy long hair, looking very white and pale, some with thick-framed glasses and others with black boots, which was a little odd for neon pink Fort Lauderdale. But it was in January, so, hey, OK. We finally asked one of these people what was going on, and we were told there was a heavy metal music festival cruise departing from the port. Those people were going to have a blast! Us? No, ***hells to the no***, would we want to be on that cruise. But our friend Mary would! In fact, she finagled a gig teaching yoga on Motorhead's Motorboat Cruise, a savvy way to trade skills for a festival ticket. (That fast-forward in ***Operation Big Fun*** will be covered in *Chapter 7: The Vend Life*).

But we have gone on a very funky Jam Cruise, and that was pretty awesome! Not only was the lineup killer (Bootsy Collins, Thievery Corporation, Dumpstaphunk and so many more), but everyone was a friend. It was an entire cruise ship filled with people a lot like us: Funky, who enjoy dressing up in fun costumes, who have a lot of energy, who like to laugh, who dance and smile to funky music and, importantly, did not seem intent on stealing any of our shit, if we had any lying around. Everyone paid the hefty $1,000+ ticket, so most people onboard were working types like we were. It was so easy to make friends.

These new friends will quickly become even closer to you that some of your family members. (For Phish fans, it's known as your "***phamily***.") Simply put, you choose to have these people in your life, and they earn their spot there. That's why it's so natural to call each other "brother" and "sister" at music festivals. It's a genuine feeling that everyone is part of a big family of people who are alike in that they, too, understand the power of love.

Look, let's be realistic for a minute. People aren't always your type at music festivals. If you are a ***wook***, you may turn your nose up at the weekend warriors who sets up with their preppy friends next to you in the campground, and vice versa. Like that lady in the Gators outfit in the front row of our first festival – we weren't similar people. But we've learned a lot since then, and now we recommend finding a friend in everyone!

But how, you ask? Oh, you're an adult now and it's *so hard* to find new friends? Oh, contraire!

***Introduce yourself to those around you.*** This is simple polite friendliness, but it's also vital for your safety as well. If some sort of shit hits the fan, you will need to rely on those around you to help in some way. Or at least you need to know who you possible COULD ask for help.

**Left, Phish at Jazz Fest and a pair of sunglasses found in the ocean.**

In this digital day and age, people get shy about "putting themselves out there" in person to befriend others. Let that go! Tell the person your name and ask theirs. Then, actually try to remember their names. It's pretty simple. This is what life is all about. Did you forget because your mind is like an open sieve? Welcome to the club. You can try to remember their name by immediately thinking of another person with the same name, or you can honestly just ask forgiveness and request they repeat it before parting. In general, it is so rare that folks put energy into remembering other people's names that we find new friends are really honored when we remember their name. They think that maybe we're worth remembering as well.

There are some other tools we can suggest to help you to make new friends. First, we always bring a small notebook to a festival and write down as much as we can remember at the end or beginning of each day. This includes the names of new friends as well as funny incidents that will make us smile later. Some of our friends will carry a very small notebook with them at all times so they can also write down set lists of the songs of their favorite musicians as the concert occur. This is a great idea, if you have the right frame of mind at the time, because that music – being the priority, you know – will be much-discussed back at camp later in the evening.

One festival, perhaps it was another one of those magical Wanees, we found myself dancing in the crowd to one of the Grateful Dead incarnations. Our friends and we (*Edit: Still hanging on to this first-person plural, nice)* had separated, and the spot where we were standing in the packed crowd turned out to be reserved legitimately for someone else's friend. So, we stumbled through the crowd until we found another friend we knew. She had a blanket set up, so there was a little extra room for us. (Heather gave us a bottle of water, too. Thanks girl!)

That's when we met Dave, who stumbled on to the blanket and also knew Heather somehow. Fast-forward two years, and we're outside of a bar, six hours by car from that blanket, in Fort Lauderdale during a break of a Grateful Dead cover band. Hmm, that guy looked familiar. Somehow, from the back of our memories, we remembered his name. Turns out we lived just a few minutes from each other! And when he sold his house and needed a place to live before moving across the country to be with the love of his life, we rented a room to him. We had a fun month listening to music and laughing, and it never would have happened had we not taken the energy to introduce ourselves and remember one another. Now, even living miles away, we still keep in touch and support one another like good friends do.

Social media is also super-helpful when it comes to remembering new friends. Not always, but often there is cell phone reception at music festivals. Be careful about bringing along your cell phone to the concert, however; those are known to be dropped and/or disappear.

**Right, our fabulous ginger friend Shelly sold us an iPhone once. But that has nothing to do with why we think she is one of the funniest people around. Take note of the layers, people. Layers.**

But if you brought your device to the show, type in your new friend's name and befriend them on whatever social media platform you use. Sometimes after the fest, we'll post pictures and tag who we know – then other friends of theirs who we had met will connect with us through those photos. We've greatly expanded our ***framily*** in this simple yet modern way.

As easy as it may be at a music festival, don't let your brain turn to mush ... if for no other reason than people aren't really quick to befriend dumb-dumbs. Stay sharp, fool! Our favorite people at music festivals make us smile and laugh with their wit. Our friend Jon used to dress up at night with LED Light Up wire like a skeleton around his body and dance like a fool. He was hilarious! Our friend Jason can make us giggle for hours around the campfire with his jokes and impressive shadow hand puppets. Get Fritzy to noodle-dance around us and we're sure to be smiling.

The best way to remember someone? Take the time to enjoy a special moment with them. Make someone laugh. Let them make you laugh. Help them. Ask to borrow something (like an air mattress pump? Geez, everyone forgets that) and then – gasp! – return it unbroken. At music festivals, ***you have the time*** it takes to get to know someone. Don't avoid human connection outside your small, existing social circle; making new friends one of the best things in the world. (*Edit: Don't make us go down that hippie hole of love again! We'll do it! We'll do it!)* Compliment someone's tapestry. Been to the town boasted on their T-shirt? Talk to them about it. You may be surprised at how much you have in common. But first you have to talk to them; then you can remember them.

Befriend the folks who are camped around you, but definitely <u>introduce yourself to the people who end up rooted around you in a crowd</u>. Crowds are funny. Unless you have a real game plan (often involving riding the rail, as previously discussed), everyone just sort-of wanders in and decides that they are going to stand in a particular spot for the next hour or two for a concert. Say hi.

We already discussed the importance of being cool in the crowd, but in the context of crowd dynamics. Another reason to not be territorial is because it's easier to make friends and have a good time this way. Sometimes people will be standing too close to you. You've got some options, but one shouldn't be to get pissed. It's ***Operation Big Fun*** here. Chill out. ***Two wrongs don't make a right.***

Here's an example: At a Phil Lesh & Friends concert in Orlando years ago, some random guy freaked out near us. "You aren't the real hippies! You aren't REAL hippies!" he suddenly yelled, pointing at random young people around him who, obviously, well post-dated the Woodstock era. The rest of the crowd had a couple of options to deal with this guy. But what was the fastest way to get back to enjoying the music, which, remember, is why we are all there? Had we defensively attacked him back, a fight could have ensued. Had we called over security, other problems might have arisen. That's not what it's all about. Instead, we calmed him down. We were his friends. He settled down. End of story. Jam on.

Of course, not everyone is going to get the memo here. I remember one year at Wanee Festival, we had neighbors at camp who were blasting death metal music very loudly, all the time. What a bummer! We were taking a lovely solar shower when a song came on with lyrics that sweetly screamed, "I WANT TO FUCK YOU LIKE I'M NEVER GONNA SEE YOU AGAINNNNNNNN!" Now that's love. We tried numerous times to politely ask them to turn the music down. It didn't work. One time, we covertly ran over to their camp and turned the music off, much to the delight of our friends. That golden silence didn't last long, alas.

Don't be that neighbor! Keep your music down. Shockingly, it might not be everyone's cup of tea. (*Edit: Really, who doesn't like a little Jerry Garcia Band in the morning?)* Keep your merriment to a respectful level. Play a little music around the campfire, sing and laugh, but don't bang more than one drum anywhere but at the drum circle (which is usually located far away from the stages and well worth a late-night visit!).

Even though the music is the priority, camp is really where friendships blossom at a festival. There's nothing quite like the late-night ***yucks*** around a fire. Our friends will pick-and-grin for hours. The first year we met our festival family, there was a guy who was simply a curmudgeon. We'll leave out his name – we would like to call him simply ***The Bundle Bandit*** – but his girlfriend's name was Dixie and he wore a hat that read, "My Dixie's wrecked." Get it? "My dick's erect." But we read it like: My girlfriend, whose name is Dixie, is wrecked. And I remember Dixie was a sweet woman who seemed a little uncomfortable in the scene but pleasant enough. Not wrecked in any way! What an ass.

Anyway, that's not even the story. One night, it was really, really cold so about a dozen of us were huddled around the fire, talking and laughing. This guy actually brought a lot of firewood, which was pretty cool and highly encouraged for everyone reading this manual. But at one point in the evening, who knows or cares how, he got really annoyed at us. Maybe we were teasing him about something? We can't remember. We mean, we remember Jonathan (who, we might add, is sober and impressively successful now) dropping his pants and shuffling around the camp in his underwear, clowning around. We remember laughing until tears, and we also remember ***The Bundle Bandit*** grabbing all the firewood he had brought and throwing it back in his truck so that we couldn't burn it. This made us laugh even louder as Jo came up with his nickname. Thankfully another friend soon arrived as we explained, with tears of laughter streaming down our faces, how ***The Bundle Bandit*** made off with our heat. The wood was replaced immediately, and that guy had officially declared he would no longer be our friend.

How did our fire stay lit? Here's an important part of why it is worth an entire chapter on the importance of finding a friend in everyone: Your friends look out for you, allowing you a support system and safety net of well-meaning and loving individuals. In turn, this comfortable environment lets us relax fully without fear of judgment and instead help. It's another reason why music festivals are so beautiful and healing. They warm the sole ... of your sneaker if you're sitting too close the fire! Ha ha! But seriously, it was Michael (rest in peace, buddy) who ran up to store to buy a bundle of firewood so we could all stay up later and drink whiskey and laugh and continue the party.

Your friends help along the way, and in return, you help when you can. It's that simple. There are a lot of unspoken rules you're hopefully picking up by reading this manual, but it can all come down to being a good, honest person and then you are rewarded for it. ***Good vibes only***.

# Chapter 5:
# Foodstuffs = Fuel

What kind of ***festy foodie*** are you? Chances are you're somewhere in between the two extremes: those who are really, really into food and those who forget to eat.

God bless those folks who come to festivals with huge coolers packed full of food. They simply cook all weekend. It's wonderful to befriend one of these "music" fans, because they often have a massive amount of food, as well as a grill or smoker. These ***phat cats*** will be likely wearing an apron around their enlarged bellies, sweating and talking a lot about food, because this is how they relate best in a group setting. These beautiful people are givers, but usually also pro-meat, which we're not into but that's OK. Some of our friends have entire conversations about bacon or steaks and/or the merits of bacon on top of steaks. So usually food is a good choice in conversation for these types. And it's wise to find a friend in these ***festy foodies***, because they've got what you need. Forget your ketchup or ran out of ice? If you're anything like us, you – gasp! – don't always have your act together and condiments are forgotten.

But try not to be on the other end of the food spectrum. These folks are simply the spun-out junkies who can't really remember to eat when they party too hard. They're often alcoholics, frankly, skinny with unbrushed teeth. They didn't pack any food, and they spent all their money on booze and/or drugs. So, they're too spun out to eat. By the way, when these folks are out late at night, they are known fondly as ***spunions***. But they're also good people, and no one wants to forget about a member of the ***framily***. Often the Mommy types will make themselves known here, acting as intermediaries between the spunion and Chef Meats-A-Lot. See how the ***framily*** comes together?

By the way, this writing team has both made delicious gourmet meals AND have forgotten to eat!

The problem with these extremes, of course, is that they are missing the most important part of the music festival: Music is the priority! Although it's great to eat well and feed your friends, eating during a music festival is all about efficiency. ***Food is the fuel*** that keeps you going during the long weekend of running around, dancing and laughing. It's vital to eat, but not so much that you are missing what you've paid for. Look, you can call all your friends up and set up camp in a state park for the weekend and eat to your heart's content. That's not what you've paid a couple hundred of your hard-earned dollars to do.

**Right, we were all pretty impressed with Owen's awesome omelets at Camp Where's My?**

In the early days, we used to be a festy foodie – not the big-bellied, meaty type, of course, but a festy foodie nonetheless. When the festival was approaching, we would sit down with a scrap of paper and list in detail all the meals we would make each day: French toast, chili, veggie burgers with all the ***fixin's***, bagels with peanut butter and slices of apple, homemade hummus with pre-cut vegetables, hard cheese and crackers, you name it. Then, as previously discussed, we would create a list of groceries to buy, another list of ingredients we already owned but wanted to bring and yet another list of what we needed to do to prepare the foodstuffs as much as possible before the actual festival.

The planning kept costs low, but that's simply too much work for a weekend of fun!

Food, for many, is an extension of the party. Those who go to Jazz Fest in New Orleans each year know what we're talking about. No doubt that when we took our ex-boyfriend for his first Jazz Fest, he was more excited about the plate of steaming oysters that wafted past us in the crowd than most of the musicians we saw (*Edit: Notice the use of the prefix "ex."*). But those oysters weren't cheap, and you can spend a lot of money buying food at vendors. Choose wisely.

Here's a general truism about food vendors: ***The bigger the dreadlocks, the tastier the grub***. Avoid the places that look like they came straight from the county fair, like the boring pizza places that scream at you with their neon signs. Those will just make you feel ill, guaranteed. And the place probably won't be run by hippies either. Spend money on the places that are unique: We've had amazing and memorable homemade sugar donuts, a spicy vegetable noodle dish and green groovy smoothies at festivals. These places are staffed by people who are or could be your friends, and they want you to be happy with their food. They put love in every bite. It's delicious.

Our friend Louie runs a food booth that sells ***Jerry rolls***, which are basically really big egg rolls. You order it and he yells "Jerrrraaaaayyyyy!" like you used to hear at Dead shows. Our friend Auggie worked with him for a while. It was pretty awesome of Lou to let Auggie have a break so we could dance to String Cheese Incident covering Earth, Wind and Fire at Lock'n Fest one year. Damn that was fun. Louie even gifted us a sandwich, and we were dancing and eating a Jerry roll at the same time. We mean, really, does it get any better? Thanks, Falafel Louie. Shout out to you. He also has sweat lodges, by the way, although we were never in town when he put them on. The point is, eating at one of these spots is, indeed, an extension of the festival.

There are some foods, like Jerry rolls, that are just a wonderful part of the festival and shouldn't be missed. Those oysters at Jazz Fest weren't the only memorable food there. WWOZ, the venerable radio station in New Orleans, sells ***Mango Freezes*** as a fundraiser during Jazz Fest. By all means, buy one. By all means, bring a small plastic bottle of rum in your boot and add it generously to the Mango Freeze. Our friend Bradley taught us this. Thanks Brad!

Just avoid too much fried food. Yes, it's call a festival but that doesn't mean you should have fried chicken legs and onion rings followed by fried Oreos. Remember, the idea is to not feel like complete shit at the end of the weekend. If you plan your intake smartly, you'll be ready to go for another festival the next weekend. We had a year when we traveled to festivals for three-straight-months-worth of weekends, with full-time work in between. We felt like champs: We came home, did laundry, made money, packed appropriately and left town. On repeat, baby!

However, buying all your foodstuffs can add up. Our main goal at a music festival is to recoup the money spent on the ticket or, if that fails, not spend a whole lot more. Like sneaking in that rum: It makes a lot more economic sense than buying daiquiris all day. (*Edit: To be truthful, we buy daiquiris and double up with that rum. It is New Orleans, after all.)* We're not cheap; we just prefer to spend money on tickets instead of booze or crappy meals. So that's why we were planning out our meals so carefully. But now we do it a little smarter, and you can too.

First, <u>do not bring more food that you will eat</u>. Why? It's a waste of money. It's pretty easy to go to the grocery store and get a whole lot of everything because you think you'll sit around and eat all weekend. But you won't. When you buy too much, you'll have to pack it all back in the car at the end of the weekend. And you'll need that extra room, because it's extra challenging to stuff everything back in the way you did with a clear head in your driveway. Trust us here. It is a very good idea to think out your meals before you go.

**Above, we interrupt this regularly scheduled guide for this very special announcement from Flava Flav of Public Enemy: YEAAAAAAAAAHHHHHHH BOOOOOOOOIIIIIII. Now you can return to your reading enjoyment.**

But unlike we did in our original belabored planning days, don't plan on meals that take a long time to cook. Look in your refrigerator. Do you have leftovers? If you do, bring them to reheat. That will save money and time. ***Look at the schedule when planning meals***.

If you are really looking forward to the headliner on Saturday, maybe you should plan to buy a Jerry roll that evening so you won't have to walk back to camp and potentially miss part of the show.

In fact, most of the meals should be on the go. Heat and serve is the answer: Veggie burgers, a can of soup, anything that is nutritious, hot and fast will be your best meal choice. Try to get food that won't require too much ice; that can be hard to come by if you're not around when the guy selling ice from his truck swings by your camp. You won't want to lug ice back to camp from the store, either.

We bring two small coolers: one for drinks, one for food. That way, we can keep as much ice cold as possible (since we won't be digging around with the top open for a stray beer). Also, we will have a backup in case of a ***cooler failure***. What is that, you ask?

At Gathering of the Vibes one year, we ended up traveling with a boyfriend at the time and his two friends. We went to a farmer's market and scored some really amazing peaches, and then we filled up a big cooler with all kinds of foods for everyone. We are vegetarian, and we were nothing short of aghast when we opened the cooler the next day to discover that one of the friends had let his bloody meat seep all over the rest of the food. It was poor ***cooler etiquette*** and simply bad form as a campmate. All the food was ruined, especially our veggie burgers. We survived on juicy peaches the entire weekend (not the worst thing), but of course the guy felt bad. Not only did he gross us out, he potentially got everyone else ill. It's worth noting here that this guy was about 300 pounds and purchased a pink, kids-size tent to sleep in, so all weekend when he was asleep his legs and entire bottom half of his rotund body were sticking out in the elements. What goes around really does come around.

Those peaches were a good idea (we ended up grilling them!), because food is fuel. Avoid bringing too many chips and cookies. Junk isn't the answer. When you arrive back to camp after a long day of hoofing it from stage to stage, you will want something warm and filling in your belly. ***Do your future self a favor*** and pack good food.

In fact, pack a lot of healthy snacks like fruit, nuts and cheese in wax. All festivals involve making your way from the campground through the security gate to the music (We talk more about this process in *Chapter 9: Life On The Road*), and in general, security guards are looking for drugs and booze. They're not going to confiscate your apple. Although, one time at Sunfest in West Palm Beach, they told us that we couldn't bring an apple in. So, we said, OK, and looked innocently at the guard. Then we slowly removed the apple from our bag and took a bite. We continued to make eye contact as we took another bite. And another, right in line. We were four, calculated bites in before the guard rolled her eyes and let us through the gate. We were going to stand there and eat that entire thing, just to prove to them how silly their rule was. Did they think we would throw it at a musician? No, they wanted us to be so hungry that we would buy something to eat. We did anyway: we love $3 roasted corn.

But you don't want to be hungry (that will distract you from your priority!), and Mom was right: Breakfast is important! At music festivals, live acts do not generally start until 11 a.m. or noon, so the organizers give you time to get over a hangover and eat a hearty breakfast. ***Bring coffee*** for the morning and energy drinks for the evening. Have a big breakfast. Do not worry about calories this weekend, because you will be dancing until dawn, if all goes according to plan. If you are going to cook something fancy, breakfast is the meal to do it.

**Left, a hangover.**

My friends like to plan a potluck brunch one day, and it's a fantastic idea. Communal meals are a fun way to connect with your friends and share the fun of the festival, which can get crazy (understatement). Potluck meals need to be made that morning or pre-made but without the need for refrigeration. My friends Bob and Elizabeth celebrated the start of their short-lived marriage at an Orange Blossom Jamboree, and we made dozens of vegan cupcakes that didn't need refrigeration but were moist and delicious for their reception. Then we gifted them the ridiculously large Tupperware containers we brought them in so that we didn't have to pack them back in our Volkswagen Beetle. Because packing in and out is a major part of the festival experience, and what you pack and what you forget can make or break the entire weekend.

# Chapter 6: What to Bring and What Not to Bring

When we attended our first New Orleans Jazz & Heritage Festival, we called up our friend Kate who had gone for years and asked her what to bring. "Bring rain boots and a jacket, regardless of the forecast," she said. It was the smartest advice we had ever received. That year, it rained so much that the race track had turned into a shitty (literally), muddy mess, stranding most participants far away from the stages, the food vendors, the bathrooms and, simply, the fun. However, we wore tall rain boots and sloshed straight through the funk to wherever we wanted to go. We made friends with strangers by delivering them food so they didn't have to ruin their shoes in the mud. Our rain jackets kept us warm and dry during shows, so we didn't have to miss the music. Everything was perfect, because we packed the right things.

**Below, the mucky, shitty field of Jazz Fest after a heavy rainfall. Kate was SO RIGHT. Bring boots (and hats!).**

Knowing what to bring – and what not to bring – cannot be overstated. Thus, it's also a source of major stress when you're getting ready to go. It's easy to pack everything except the kitchen sink, but then you're overwhelmed with possessions. Remember all those Mexican blankets we ended up having to lug across the festival grounds to the friends giving us a ride home? We really wished we hadn't brought those. (However, they did make for a comfy floor to lounge on in the returning RV!) It's normal to think that you should bring everything, in case you'll want it, but it's smarter to plan your festival out so that you only bring what you need.

So let's plan it out, shall we?:

Clothes: You'll need ***festy fashions***, no doubt about it. Whether you are male or female, you'll need looks that are colorful, comfortable and fun. Vendors can help you create a wardrobe of festy fashions, with cool T-shirts and hippie dresses, if you don't already own these items. But the point is, the clothes you wear at the festival can be very different from those you feel you need to wear in "normal" life.

One year, we were heading to the Magnolia Festival straight from work. We were a marketing team working at a local nonprofit at the time, and we had planned a press conference after securing a new computer lab for a rural club in central Florida. We were wearing black pants suit and heels (*Edit: Here comes the first-person plural writing team in black, galaxy defenders!),* and a few state representatives came and pictures were taken. Our car was already packed for the festival, so we left straight from the press conference. Wiping the makeup from our face(s) at a rest stop along the way, we changed from the black pants suit into a bright red hemp tank dress that hung to the ground. We rolled something to smoke and made it to the festival in time to set up camp before the awesome funk band Dumpstaphunk came on stage. Getting out of the suit and into something colorful, comfortable and fun was the first step of the festival transformation.

Now is the time to wear your tie-dye t-shirts, the dress with pictures of kittens in space, those neon purple leggings with a yellow tutu, your dad's old jeans with the cool patches – anything that will make others smile. One piece of advice for ladies: Avoid overalls or jumpers that will be problematic in the bathroom. The last thing you want to do is spend extra time in a Port-O-John undressing. Ugh.

Express your creativity through your clothes at a festival. Your clothes should be fun to pack, so make sure you are smiling in your bedroom as you are getting ready to leave. At a fest, no one is judging you, and that's part of what makes these events so special. No need for makeup. No need for worrying about what you've got. No ***festy fashions***? Don't worry about it. If anyone is going to judge you by your clothes, that's their problem. Relax. That's the whole point.

While you are packing your clothes, though, be sure to check the weather. Chances are it will be warm during the day and cool in the evenings. You won't want to be a prima donna and change clothes all the time; create outfits with layers so that you'll look funky and be comfortable. The more comfortable you are, the more fun you'll have. Leave the tight jeans at home! Pack rain gear, a bathing suit and super-warm clothes. One year at the Wanee Festival (in April), it dropped down to freezing. Luckily, we had packed a wool toque and a sweater. Bring layers so you're prepared for hot, cold, rain and wind. You won't over pack if you think out what you want to wear each day, but bringing a few extra pieces if you sweat or stink it up. Hey, it happens.

Camp: If you are going with friends, consider splitting up the camp equipment responsibilities. Have one person bring the stove and propane, another bring a table, another bring tarps or firewood. Make it clear who is doing what, however; when your friends are stoners, they tend to forget important things. Personally, even though we often camp with a large group of friends, we tend to stay self-sufficient and bring everything we need.

It's also a really good idea to have one of these friends arrive super-early, days early if possible. Staking claim to land as close to the security gates as possible is crucial to preserving energy in the future. When planning with your crew, get the lay of the land (and maybe pack a bicycle, too!).

It's nice to have these camp items pre-packed, especially if you find yourself going to a lot of festivals in a season. We've tried a few options: black milk crates are easy to top-load in and out of the car, but the holes can make things inside dirty. We packed camping stuff in large, waterproof Tupperware-style bins, and those are a little bulkier but better. Just stack 'em in the garage or shed in between shows. You'll be halfway packed even before you buy your ticket.

There are things you'll always want:

* A tent and warm sleeping bag or warm blankets, even if it's the middle of summer
* A pillow and an air mattress (and a battery-operated pump!)
* A camping stove with a couple small propane canisters
* A pot, wooden spoon, plate, bowl and utensils (We encourage you to avoid waste and reuse a plate and utensils instead of buying disposables. It doesn't take a lot of time to clean up after a meal, and you'll feel better not creating a big heap of trash.) Also, bring some dish soap, a sponge and a dish towel.
* A flashlight or headlamp, or both, with batteries that are working
* A few tarps: One for underneath the tent and one to be fashioned over the tent for shade or rain protection
* A solar shower, clothesline, clothes pins, and a few tapestries for the ***hippie shower***
* A camping chair to put around the fire to join your friends late-night after the show to discuss the day

But that's really just the basics. ***Camp landmarks*** are crucial and also a way to create space. Many festivals take place in large, open fields with few landmarks, and you'll need to figure out a way to stake your land quickly and get your bearings later. Your friends will ask you where you are camped, and the directions will say something like, "You know where the big white van with the Jerry Garcia flag? Pass that on the dirt road and you'll see a few tie-dyed lawn ornament flowers. Keep walking and look for the neon lights up in the trees. We're back there, behind the dancing bear tapestry." Our friends often have a large sign with the name of our camp, which varies. It's often called ***Camp Where's My?*** because you will be surprised how often you are hunched over, looking in your plastic bins for that thing that you know you packed and where the heck is it? We like to bring one of those $1 plastic pinwheels, to stick in the dirt out front of our tent to announce that we are, oh yes, ready to party.

Personal items: We'll discuss all the toys worth bringing in *Chapter 8: Making it Happen*, because there's a lot of fun to be had with the things you bring.

So, you'll want to bring a bag to put all these things in. Deciding on the type of bag you want to bring takes research. Some festivals are sticklers about what types of bags you can bring through security, and the rules can change by the day. We like having a backpack, and the Camelbak was a game-changer. For those who aren't in the know, a Camelbak is a backpack that has a water bladder and drinking hose in a separate section of the bag. Dehydration is a big deal at music festivals.

In fact, we are big, big fans of bringing in water, but some security guards like to think they're the TSA. In general, the rule is you can bring in ***one, unopened bottle of water***. To most people, this means an 8-oz. bottle, but let's get real. That is not enough to keep you rockin' for hours, especially if you are drinking alcohol, which dehydrates you further. More often than not, the first day of the festival, the security guards are really lax and don't care if you bring water in a water bottle, once they are sure the clear liquid isn't a big jug of vodka. But then the second day, sometime in the afternoon, they act like bringing in water is a criminal act and get righteous about it. This should only encourage you to get more creative.

We do not encourage bringing small plastic bottles of water to festivals, because this creates an amazing amount of waste. Plus, they are just plain unsatisfying! After dancing like a maniac for hours, you need a big gulp. So, one option is bringing in an empty Camelbak and a full, unopened gallon of water. We befriend a vendor and store the gallon of water behind their tent, filling the Camelbak bladder whenever necessary.

However, lately, there have been a few festivals that are banning all backpacks, period. What a major bummer when we were turned away from the gates of SunFest in West Palm Beach, Florida as the Bangles played "Eternal Flame" in the distance. As we literally ran back to the car to find a cloth grocery bag to use to carry a sweater, granola bar and other carefully packed items, we thought, "Well, there goes the one time we'll ever hear that song live." Because why the hell would we ever pay to see the Bangles? And why the hell do we know every word to that song?

**Left, Julie on Jam Cruise! It pays to have friends with balconies. It also pays to have a friend like Julie who energetically paves a path ahead for making the world a better place. Note the tattoo of Tattoo.**

What made a backpack that much worse than a shoulder bag was totally unclear. Unreasonable rules are totally outrageous. But the bottom line is, this is the only time these lame security guards have any sort of authority in their lives. They have to use whatever they can.

Thus, when packing for a music festival, be sure to bring a variety of ***day bags***. Be sure that these bags are filled with full knowledge they will be searched. Planning on sneaking a beer in? Do not put it in the bag, fool. Alcohol is the main thing they are looking for. Put that can in the back of your pants waistband, right on your back, and geez, really wait until you are quite far from the gate before pulling it out and celebrating that you snuck it through in the first place!

At the Gorge, our friend gave us an Altoid mint with an illegal substance on it. It was the kind of substance that would lead to big-eye pupils and giggles for approximately eight hours. We put this in a cellophane wrapper from a cigarette box and stashed it in a little pocket in our backpack. When the security guard pulled it out in an accusatory fashion, we self-righteously said, "It is a MINT!" And we got through, mint and all.

**Right, Megan, Andrew and Steve walking down to The Gorge.**
**Not pictured: Ray, who was holding down HQ, surely.**

One way to beat the system is to put something that looks very suspicious at the top of the bag. It is unlikely, though not impossible, that the security guard is going to really rip the entire bag apart. Once they check one or two things, they really just want to keep the line moving. We store our earplugs in a small plastic container that indeed looks like someplace where someone would put drugs. Almost every time we hit the gate, a guard will pull that out with this "Gotcha!" face, only to realize that, excuse us, we are responsible and care for ourselves. They usually don't look at anything else. ***Distraction*** is the name of the game at the security gate. Sneaking in beers in your parka pocket? Bring a big blanket and open it and shake it in front of them with a face that says, "I am completely open and transparent!" This doesn't always work, but it usually does.

What should you bring in this ***day bag***, besides contraband? We recommend:

- A lighter – Notice we do NOT encourage you to bring in cigarettes. They are disgusting and you should quit if you smoke them. But lighters? You'll definitely want one of those.
- Lip balm
- The schedule, because you will look at it a million times. Do NOT think you are going to remember which band is playing where and when. You simply will not.

- A layer of clothes, like a sweatshirt or something. This will allow you to stay out longer, while your friends are running back to camp to get warm. This is a fine line when it comes to packing, of course; you don't want to be lugging too much around.
- Some gum or mints. They don't have to be laced with anything, but it's especially nice when it's a dusty scene. Gum is also a heavenly thing to share with those around you.
- Toys of the day, to be discussed in *Chapter 8*.

Back at camp, you'll want some other personal items as well. Bring vitamins and definitely bring Vitamin C. Did you know that breathing cigarette smoke depletes this vitamin, also known as "nature's antibiotic"? Remember all those health tips earlier in this manual, and chew 500 milligrams of Vitamin C three times a day during the festival. (This will also prevent UTIs, ladies!)

Bring toiletries in a bag that can be slung over the shoulder and can hang easily on a hook in a sketchy shower. You're already familiar with a ***hippie shower***; bring everything you need for that.

It's also a good idea to bring a roll of toilet paper in a Ziploc bag. When you visit the toilet for a #2 in the morning after that big, strong cup of coffee, you'll feel like a champ when you're prepared even though the roll is empty. Feeling like a champ in a Port-O-John, oh yeah. That's the stuff.

All personal items you bring, of course, are simply ways that you care for yourself. But please don't get crazy. Is that aluminum in your deodorant? You'll have the government spying on you in no time. It's like those pregnant hippie girls who are planning on a natural childbirth. Sisters, that's when you WANT the drugs. (*Edit: Credit goes to Julie for that laugh.)*

<u>Transport</u>: Getting around at a festival is also your responsibility. If nothing else, think about your shoes. In fact, there's an appropriate Phish lyric here: ***Whatever you do, take care of your shoes***. Are you the type of hippie who never wears shoes? That's not a good idea at a music festival. Look around! There's Drunky McSkunky breaking a bottle on the ground. Now he dropped his half-eaten sandwich. Now he's puking. Uh-oh, he just fell down. Sure, it's daytime now and you see him enough to avoid his path. But what about after the sun sets? Do you really want to follow in his footsteps, literally?

One year, Langerado was held at Big Cypress in the Everglades. As seasoned festival-goers, we went online to print out the music schedule and look at the grounds to get an idea of the venue since we hadn't been there. The organizers posted a note encouraging festival-goers to wear closed-toe shoes and not make open camp fires. The guy we were dating at the time was incensed! He made a big fuss about not being about to wear flip-flops and how he wanted to make a fire. We took their advice and purchased some super-comfortable hemp sneakers.

Fast forward to the festival: The campground was simply a cow pasture with rows of Port-O-Johns every 100 yards or so. By day, you could see and avoid the piles of cow patties and fire ant mounds; at night, however, it was a different story. You just trudged right through. Within a day, our (*Edit: loser*) guy had to visit the emergency tent with feet completely swollen from fire ant bites. Then he tried to build a fire, which in the wind almost immediately caught on the surrounding tall grasses and nearly burned down our EZ Up.

The point is, egomaniacs, organizers aren't trying to play power trips. Just like we're not. We're just trying to help!

Simply stated, wear comfortable, sturdy walking shoes. We are partial to Keens, but Tevas or any sort of day hikers will work. If you are a slow mover, it's cool; we know where you can score some sweet-ass ***rope sandals***! Having a pair of shoes that can be worn with a warm pair of socks is smart packing. Just, by all means, leave those bright white Reebok sneakers at home. You'll give us a bad flashback, dude.

At many venues, a bicycle is a great idea if you have the room to bring it. At Lock'n, our bicycle was a Godsend! We could pedal from our campsite at the top of the hill down through the vending area, known fondly as ***Shakedown Street*** (explained in full in the next chapter), right down to the music stages in five minutes. We locked up the bike (yes, bring a lock!) and boogied on in at least 30 minutes ahead of our friends who didn't have bikes.

If you bring a bike, be sure to make it a reason for people to smile! (Why? Keep reading to *Chapter 8*) We fashioned a bouquet of silk red roses to our bike basket, which we could also safely attach a can of beer without having to worry about it spilling (except for extremely bumpy terrains). Our friend Adam strung battery-powered Light Up wire through his bike spikes and connected a little bubble machine to the back, so he would leave silly, soapy fun in his wake.

Bikes have down sides as well. For one, they can be stolen. Many friends who brought bikes to Wanee and left them at their camps for the night awoke to find them missing. Always lock them! Of course, this in itself can backfire. At that same Lock'n, Adam locked his bike to ours to see music and then we stood in front of our bikes for at least 20 minutes trying to unlock that damn thing. We were about to give up when it suddenly unlocked. Read into this moment what you will.

Motorized dirt bikes are also a great thing to bring. Slightly harder to steal and obviously faster and more dangerous with each additional alcoholic beverage, dirt bikes are also even less likely to be allowed in the vast majority of the festival grounds. But depending on the venue, they can get you and your friends to where you want to go quickly. That means you'll miss out on less music and also be a hero when, say, a ***Bundle Bandit*** wants to steal all the firewood and someone needs to go buy another stack.

**Above, we are not funky. Bootsy Collins, now HE IS FUNKY. Blowing our minds on Jam Cruise.**

Many venues also make a pretty penny by renting golf carts, while some festy regulars bring their own. Golf carts are awesome at festivals, so if it's in your budget we say go for it. Be sure, like your bike, you decorate it with as many crazy decorations as possible. Pump a sound system loudly with fun music, too. God bless whomever it is playing "Funkytown" on repeat and drives around the festival venue with a glittery disco ball reflecting light into campsites. Yes and yes!

# Chapter 7: The Vend Life

Every festival has at least one spot where vendors line up, selling all kinds of ***kynd*** wears and food. It is known fondly as ***Shakedown Street***, named after, of course, the groovy Grateful Dead song that describes the place as the "heart of the town." And indeed, there is a lot of shakin' on Shakedown Streets at music festivals.

What do you want to buy? A tie-dye shirt? A hemp backpack? A crystal or a hammock? Hey, we know! Let's get you in a pair of ***rope sandals***!

We first experienced an inside look at the Vend Life while (*Edit: collectively*) dating a guy who sold bamboo lights. In fact, this is how we met. One festival, there came a downpour and we ran into the nearest tent. It happened to be this guy's tent, with bamboo lights strung around the perimeter, and we started talking. A few months later, we met each other again in the town where we happened to both live and he asked us out repeatedly until we finally acquiesced.

**Left, the bamboo lights are cool, failed relationship and all.**

Fast forward 30 seconds, which is unfortunately about as long as we think out the start of long-term relationships, and he's living at our place. The backyard quickly transformed into a production studio for these bamboo lights, especially when festival season kicked into high gear. He'd be up late at night, connecting lights and finishing his handmade designs, which, unlike the actual relationship, were pretty cool. We had them hanging all around the house.

We were happy to get a free ticket in exchange for working his tent for part of the day. We would arrive a day earlier than the vast majority of festivalgoers to set up shop. That meant driving up to the vending area and unloading a trailer of goods. We would hang these lights around an EZ Up with bungee cords, set up a few tables and drape tapestries over it. We would usually bring a rug from the house and create a comfortable place to stand, since standing on dirt (or mud) all day hurt the back after a while.

So, not to make a whole commercial or anything, but for those who haven't seen one of these bamboo lights, let us break the creative process down. Our ex would start by harvesting giant thorny bamboo stalks from nearby yards and let it cure. Then he'd cut and core the bamboo, next using a spiral drill bit to create a pattern of holes in the bamboo and stuff LED string lights in the hollowed-out middle. It was a labor-intensive process. During the day, these bamboo lights were pretty and all, but at night they really came alive.

At festivals, you could see the glow from across Shakedown. ***Spunions*** would come like moths to a flame. We talked to all kinds of crazies who were mesmerized by the products. Some of them even bought some, if they were sober enough to manage monetary transactions.

What was especially nice about being a vendor is that often it's possible to sleep close to (or in!) the booth. This means you never have to deal with security, because ***Shakedown Street*** is almost always on the other side of the security gate from camping. You can drink your own beers at the concert and drink water from your own water bottle. Often times, vendors will barter with one another or sell their goods at a reduced rate. There are a lot of perks.

But it's work. Let's face it, festivals are really amazing because they let you escape from being the working stiff you normally are. It's one thing to hustle day and night to make enough money to go have fun; it's another thing to interrupt your fun to hustle. Some people are always hustling. Those people are the best ones to live the Vend Life.

Those bamboo lights weren't our only vending experience. We did a few shows with Magoo, who sold those ***rope sandals*** and Alex Gray shirts, along with what are known as ***lot shirts***. There are many, many kinds of lot shirts, and not all are the same. You get what you pay for from the guy who is hustling in the lot or around the campground. Shirts that good guys like Magoo sells are fine quality and usually way cooler designs than what one would buy from the official ***merch tent.*** Magoo had some cool artwork used by permission from artists like Blake Wiley and catchy phrases like Hunter S. Thompson's "Buy the ticket, take the ride."

**Right, the beloved Magoo and a stuffed monkey doppelgänger to Joshua's buddy, D'Angelo.**

We always prefer souvenirs from rad shops on ***Shakedown Street*** to the official band ***merch***. One time we bought an official, merch-quality Parliament Funkadelic t-shirt and when we put it on, the hem was weirdly to one side. You know crappy shirts like those? No matter how much you pull it back, it still twists and is never quite right. Bummer.

Magoo is a great guy, and he brought us on during Lock'n to work for a few hours when bands we didn't need to see where playing. We also worked together at Sweetwater 420 festival in Atlanta; he flew us up for that and put us up in a hotel, in exchange working all weekend. That was a fantastic experience: We ate amazing Indian food and his huge

***stalker-style white van*** was hit by some mindless driver. When the cops showed up, they were surprisingly cool with the unsurprising fact that Magoo didn't have any of his paperwork together. We were going to do many more festivals together but the office job got in the way. But for a while, the Vend Life made the Fest Life happen. Magoo also generously treated us to a ***Dirty Hippy***, which are delicious. Plus, we made a little cash. Pretty sweet.

Once you're on the inside of the vending scene, you start to experience festivals in a different way. One thing we noticed at Sweetwater was how amazingly drunk everyone seemed to be. We witnessed no less than three complete face-plants on the sidewalk. Granted, they were serving delicious blueberry Sweetwater beer, but still.

*(Edit: We'd like to take this time to pay homage to all the fruity and otherwise crafty beers we have enjoyed as festivals. There are sometimes surprisingly good beer selections for sale at festivals; it is a horrible situation when it's like, Miller Lite only. Dear Lord and they won't let us take our own heady IPAs through the security gates! Try local craft beers when you can, if only for the authentic experience of it.)*

There are always a lot of ***looky-loos*** on Shakedown, and there's nothing wrong with that. Those are the people who just stroll along, oblivious that live music is playing. Oddly, for some people, music is not the priority. It's shopping. Some people come with serious shopping in mind, ready to decorate their man cave or stock up on ***festy fashions***, but most find it hard to part with their hard-earned cash. Hey, we get that. But here's a simple piece of shopping advice: If you like the item so much that you keep coming back and trying it on, and thinking about it, just buy it. We don't know why some people have to make big productions out of their lives. When it's rainy and you're trying to make a buck and everyone just comes in and mills around, it gets old.

When working a vendor's booth at a festival, it's more important than ever to be wary of ***dirtheads***. Dirtheads are the type of ***wook*** who are generally anarchists and nihilists who, basically, give no funks. They will steal from other's campsites, be mean to their dogs and lift anything they can from a vendor booth. You have to understand: Most people at festivals are all peace and love, all "hey brother," but dirtheads aren't like that. They are angry at the world. They are at a festival not for the music and the good time; they're there because they don't have anything else going on in their life and they like drugs. We're not judging; it just is what it is. There are some jolly dirtheads, but in general, they're all a little too punk rock for our tastes.

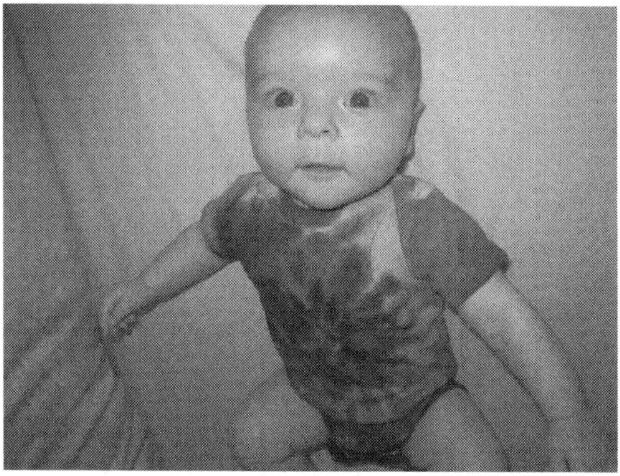

**Above, Zoe in a pretty rad tie-dye onesie, one of the many we gave as baby gifts over the years.**

When you're working at a little retail shop geared toward hippies (Magoo's official shop name is "Magoo's Cool Hippie Stuff"), you start to understand the nuances among the different kinds of people who attend a festival. Some people place great importance on buying items as proof of their memories. This writing team loves buying gifts for friends and family from ***Shakedown Street*** because in general, these unique and fun stickers, clothing and art would never be for sale in your little hometown. We encourage stocking up on ***tie-dye onesies*** for friends who are pregnant or just had a baby. Everyone thinks their baby is going to grow up to be the President of the United States until they stick 'em in a tie-dye onesie. Then it's clear: He's gonna be a stoner, just like mom and dad.

Working in a vending booth is a great way to recoup the money you spend to get to the festival or at the festival, but be aware that you'll be indeed working. Remember Louie who hooked us up with a ***Jerry Roll*** while we were dancing to Earth, Wind and Fire? We actually saw him a decade earlier, at the end of the night at the Widespread Panic New Year's Eve run. It was time to clean up, and obviously he just wanted to get the hell out of there. I really could relate – it was almost ***first light early birds*** at this point, and I was about to roll back to my hotel room. He was ordering his crew every which way, and everyone was scurrying around. We have a vivid memory of making eye contact with one of his employees as he wiped sweat from his exhausted brow. Hey, ***Jerry Rolls*** aren't made with magic, we get it. Sometimes it's laughter, and sometimes it's simply really hard work.

Folks who are regular vendors at music festivals usually set up at many, many, many venues every summer, and it can be tiring. It's also a really excellent way to make money, much better than sitting in an office all day. And unlike working in a regular retail store, it's OK to be a freak. That's worth something.

We've never worked in a food spot on Shakedown, but plenty people do. They seem to work a lot more. The key to success with the Vend Life is communicating expectations with the boss of the booth. Why are you going to the festival? Is it a summer job, where you are satisfied making money, traveling and hanging out with friends? Or do you consider the job to be a free ticket into the show? In the latter case, make sure your shifts are during bands you're not interested in or at least not during that one headliner you're dying to see. Otherwise, you'll be pissed and feel taken advantage of. *No bueno.*

If you get it right, the Vend Life is a lot of fun. I've met a lot of really cool people who are fellow vendors. Stealie Dan makes Steal Your Face ***lot shirts*** that have sports-related music puns on them. He's got a niche market for sure, music-loving sports fans. But a die-hard is a die-hard, I guess! Dan's gruff, but a good guy. When the security guards start being dicks about bringing in filled reusable water bottles (***one unopened bottle of water per person****!*)*,* Dan would let us stash an unopened gallon jug of water at his tent for frequent refills through the day. We also traded energy work for an amazing Grateful Dead dancing bear-Krishna T-shirt that has gotten many compliments during yoga classes.

We got in free to Jazz Fest one year by volunteering at the book tent. There really wasn't much to do by our shift, since everything was all set up already. But we could buy delicious local beers from their cooler for $1 and even got to meet Dennis McNaley, an author who traveled extensively with the Grateful Dead. With no other instructions, we decided to stand next to him in a handler-type manner (*Edit: that is, lingering creepily nearby*) the entire time he was signing his book to listen to the questions others were asking him. We volunteered for four hours, and then went and saw music for the rest of the day.

Here's an important thing about vendors, though: Understand what is OK and what is not. For example, Magoo is 36-years sober. While he's a cool dude who doesn't care if someone walks in with a beer (so long as they don't spill it!), it's not cool to drink on the job with him, even if that was no problem when selling bamboo lights. Stealie Dan was understandably nervous about anyone who would smoke weed near his booth. It's not OK. These folks are trying to make money in a respectable manner. It's their booth and their rules. If they say get out, then apologize and go away. They've been doing this a very long time. They know what they are doing. Respect that.

Vendors have their spot, and their spot is theirs. It's weird to work in a booth because during your shift you can't ever leave. If a ***freakazoid*** wants to talk with you for hours, you just kind of have to ... until you can get your friend to interject and save you. Don't be the ***freakazoid***. Instead, be a helpful friend; that's really the best way to get on the good side of a vendor. Ask them if they are hungry and run over to a food vendor and hook them up. Do they need to go to the bathroom? Hang out at their booth and make sure no one comes and steals stuff for five minutes. Doing this will, in general, bring rewards of free food, drink and/or laughs.

Our friend Bean Spence is a very talented artist who often has a booth up at Florida festivals, and with pleasure we'll run an errand for him or watch his booth. We had some good belly laughs ***hippie fishing***. The bait: a glow stick. At night, we attached a glow stick to the end of a fishing line and set in out in the main thoroughfare and wait for someone to bend down to pick it up. Inevitably, someone would try and the person on the other end of the line would yank it away, causing the person to either chase it or become completely confused. Then the whole crew of people in on the joke would erupt in a fit of giggles. A dollar bill is another really good bait for hippies. We had hours of good, old-fashioned fun doing this while "working."

**Above, Bean in action.**

Sometimes, personal economics are such that you need to work to get to the festival. So, do it. But getting to the festival is just the first phase of making it happen. Keep reading.

# Chapter 8: Making it Happen

You've done it! You purchased your ticket by begging, borrowing or stealing (your face) and packed your camping gear and clothing appropriately so you're self-sufficient and comfortable. You are ready with the foodstuffs and a cooler of your favorite beverages. Now it's time to make it happen.

See, everything in this manual up to this point is just the basics, my friends. Get ready to step through one of these three thresholds, also known as a ***limin*** (*Edit: Reader, please choose one):*

* Karma Wash: At the Gathering of the Vibes, campers were encouraged to walk through a small makeshift EZ-Up corridor covered with rainbow-colored streamers. Similar to a car wash that you drive through, you walk through this Karma Wash as crazy hippies pretend to "scrub" you down with

mops and bubbles so that you could be cleansed of your (presumably bad) karma.

* Alice's Rabbit Hole: This was created by the Short Cut Camp gang who we'll be talking about later in this chapter. But imagine crawling through a large PVC pipe connected to the bottom of a hanging sheet on which a tree is drawn and coming into *Through the Looking Glass* ....

* Velocitron: At Orange Blossom Jamboree, you stumble back behind the pavilion to what seems like a trailer for an 18-wheeler. As you approach, the door mysteriously opens and you find yourself inside on a metal sidewalk around which a black and white op-design-covered cylinder rotates rapidly. And somehow you walk down that sidewalk without vomiting.

Now you're on the other side of your life! Can you handle it? That's right, it's a festival. ***You help make it***! Knowing that we create our own lives – and have the ability to bring joy and success to those around us – is an understanding that helps create successful, smart and happy people. They aren't afraid to try something that may set them apart and cause people to look at them and try to figure them out. Maybe some people just won't understand you, but it is worth the risk to put a smile on other's faces.

This is what The Fest Life is all about, brothers and sisters. Let's get the world smiling!

**Left, an amazing costume at Hulaween.**

A festival is an ideal place to work on this general way of living, because it's fun! You can figure out what makes you smile, and we highly encourage you to share yourself with others. That's what sets this whole chapter apart from *Chapter 6*'s big checklist of stuff to pack. There's no checklist for what YOU are supposed to bring to make the festival experience better for you and those around you. You get to figure it out all by yourself.

For example, when we pack for a festival, we will always make sure to have two long, bubble wands filled with soap and ready for blowing. These bigger-than-your-average-bubble plastic toys cost $1 at Wal-Mart (*and we do NOT advocate shopping at Wal-Mart ever, ever although for some reason in the little town where we were living in Florida, that was the only place to find those bubble wands. And trust us, we looked.)*

For only a $1, it was unbelievable the amount of joy bubbles would bring to so many people. Children of course loved the bubbles, and that would actually get kind of annoying, we're not going to lie, because we'd be drinking beer and chilling and suddenly parents would try to drop their children off for a little free entertainment. No one is your babysitter at a festival, unless all parties agree, especially if the sole reason you choose that person is because she purchased a $1 item.

"Oh look it's the ***bubble girl*****!"** If we had a quarter for every time some dude would look at us, point and say that, we would own a lot of bubble wands. Seriously? We spend $1 and have a new identity? That is hilarious. But hey, so it is. Say it loud: We're Bubble Girls and proud! Because really, it is so fun when music is rippling through the crowd and there are so many smiles already, and just as the keyboardist starts his solo, we wave the bubble wand and a big batch of joy floats above heads with the wind. Drunks always try to pop them. Who knew what fun a little bit of soap could be.

Now, those big bubble wands made with a stick and a piece of rope, along with a bucket of dish soap? Those are really cool. It takes a special flick of the wrist to successfully close one of those huge orbs and let it lumber precariously close to trees and chairs as it slowly rises.

Our friend Craig owned a bubble gun. We just now decided to call him the Bubble Bandit. His weapon shoots a steady stream of bubbles, which is cool when it is pointed in the air but not at all cool when Craig accidently points it straight at someone. We knew we immediately had to befriend him after seeing him hug someone and point the gun negligently at the person next to his friend. It's obviously better to be the friend than the innocent bystander. He probably has no idea how careless he is with the soap until he reads this. (*Edit: Hi Craig! Are you reading this? Is anyone reading this?*)

In many ways, Craig and fellow bubblers are doing hippies a favor. It's always a good thing to force hippies to use soap.

Bubbles not ***your jam***? There is a time and place for it, we agree. There are infinite ways to spread joy. We also pack a hula hoop. For a while there, every single person on this writing team (*Edit: Insert eye roll*) was driving a Volkswagen Beetle, one of the new ones (but don't worry we were totally a cliché when it broke down at AsheFest and had to be towed down the mountain to Asheville, where, *awwww shucks,* we just had to crash with our friend

Naomi and enjoy that magical city for a few extra days while it was getting fixed over a holiday weekend). Anyway, one hula hoop was extra-large and had to be strapped to the outside of the hatchback with bungee cords. Mysteriously, no cop saw this as a special engraved invitation to search the car. Always bring a couple toys to play with. Whatever you see that makes you smile, because chances are you won't be the only one.

***Festy fashions*** is based on the idea that clothes are another way to bring smiles to people's faces. They can be purchased on ***Shakedown Street***, of course, as well as found in thrift stores and your friends' closets. It's worth the extra effort of digging into the depths of your closet. Those witty ***lot shirts***, flowy skirts and tie-dyes are simply made for smiles at music festivals. We once found a t-shirt in a Goodwill, and alas it was really a child's size, but it was a $1 so we bought and wore it anyway. It was bright red with pictures of small, silver appliances like toasters and blenders floating around the words, "Problems form alliances with appliances." Huh? We didn't really understand it either. But this kooky shirt made for great ***festy fashion***, because it was funny.

Wearing brightly colored clothing also differentiates the festival life from "normal" life. Do you work in an office? Chances are you own lots of clothing made of dark colors, relatively uncomfortable shoes and perhaps even, gasp!, a suit or two. If you plan on attending a festival, or have many under your tie-dyed belt, you'll need a completely separate wardrobe of festy fashions. If these wardrobes were in their own Venn diagram, there would be no overlapping.

**Below, Rainbow Brite. Note the pinwheel next to the tent to make it feel "homey," the beer koozie that reads, "Stay Smart" around the beer and the "Yes on 2 Legalize Marijuana" political sign.**

Wearing brightly colored clothing also differentiates the festival life from "normal" life. Do you work in an office? Chances are you own lots of clothing made of dark colors, relatively uncomfortable shoes and perhaps even, gasp!, a suit or two. If you plan on attending a festival, or have many under your tie-dyed belt, you'll need a completely separate wardrobe of festy fashions. If these wardrobes were in their own Venn diagram, there would be no overlapping.

*(Edit: We would like to add in Buddhist tangent, because we can. There is actually a "right work" philosophy that states you will be happiest in the job where you can wear whatever clothes you would want to wear naturally and never have to "put on a work outfit." Like Mr. Rogers, who would come home and immediately take off his day wear and slip into something a little more comfortable. What if Mr. Rogers could rock that sweater at work? What if ... it had Grateful Dead dancing bears on it!? What if Mr. Rogers came home and unveiled a tie-dye under his sweater?)*

We remember sitting in the second row of a big field waiting for The Allman Bros. to come on stage. We were with our friends, and, in our mind's eye, if you're ***picking up what we're putting down,*** things were starting to get a little strange. Adam's dreadlocks started to look a little like snakes. Um, the snakes were moving. Is this what Medusa was all about? We looked next to Adam and got a real eyeful. ***Festy fashion*** to the extreme: This lady next to Adam was wearing a 70's vintage polyester neon pink, green, blue and brown paisley gown. The design was pulsing. Hard. It was actually a little intense, and we actually grabbed our friend, hey thanks Robin, and got out of there.

Checking out crazy tie dyes, sparkles on skirts, ironic t-shirts – ***people-watching*** is what we're talking about, basically – is part of the festival experience. But what this writing team recommends in this guide is to be a part of the show. Find items that you enjoy and sport 'em with pride. Of course, be smart here. It's more important to dress appropriately for the weather. Pack enough layers so that you remain warm and happy. It's a fine balance to wear a look that allows you to participate in ***making the scene*** and handling the reality of camping. Don't get sick just because you want to wear that sparkly tutu even though it's cold at night. If it's cold, think more along the lines of a full-body unicorn furry suit. You don't want to be back to the grind, a week later, with the ***wook flu*** sniffles.

Before departing for a festival, when we have the time, we put some dedicated effort into thinking about clothes. If necessary, we have the ability to throw clothes in a bag and roll, but we recommend thinking it out. The main reason? It's fun! Pull out your festy fashions and creating new ***bizarro*** looks that make you smile. For example, when we discovered that the velvet hunter green blazer purchased from Goodwill actually matched the multi-colored glitter tutu discovered in the kids section of another random thrift store? Smiles for miles.

Besides the festy fashions that may seem a lot like costumes unto themselves, we also encourage actual Halloween-type costumes as well. It doesn't have to be Halloween to dress up. When it IS a Halloween and you're at a music festival, well, that is awesome! It's a smart move to mine those pop-up Halloween stores that appear each fall in strip malls. The two or three days after the big day is the time to go and score silly stuff for cheap. We once owned a huge Tupperware bin filled with wigs, glow-in-the-dark tutus and other bits and pieces of costumes. If you find deals and get creative, you won't ever have to wear the same costume twice. Members of this extensive writing team have been a space alien (*Edit: Water guns may be the best accessory for a festival, ever!),* a Native American (*Edit: We now know this is this considered cultural appropriation and we apologize, albeit sexily.*), Rainbow Brite (*Edit: We just dated ourselves.*), a Day of the Dead ghost that our friends declared was a "Dead Mary Poppins." Want to guess what vintage velvet blazer Dead Mary Poppins rocked? Hint: It also matched a certain tutu.

Earlier in the foodstuffs round up, we mentioned our friends' short-lived marriage that started with some vegan cupcakes as part of the potluck meal. At that time, we had a little extra time before the festival to donate to Making It Happen for them. Elizabeth set a theme of "Over the Rainbow" for camp and asked members of this writing team to create a sign for our camp. We painted a big rainbow on a big, white piece of wood and wrote the name of the camp over it. Then underneath we left a big space and hung an array of colorful Sharpies below so that all their friends could write well wishes underneath the rainbow, which of course was totally glitter-bombed and sealed to make shiny.

The next addition to the Over the Rainbow camp was a ***rage stick***. Rage sticks are an appropriate nickname for creative, unique artwork that is attached to a high pole that is carried through the crowd. Our friend Michael had one with a big plastic mule on it. All of them are crazy, featuring random pop characters or household items, and understandably videotapers hate them. But we think they are fun and a great way to find your friends in a big crowd.

The ***rage stick*** we made for the wedding really wasn't rage-y at all. It was an ode to love. On the top of a six-foot bamboo pole, we attached a Styrofoam heart, covered with rainbow ribbon, stuck with multi-colored pipe cleaners, bent into silly shapes, around the outside of the heart. Then, we tied some gold lamé fabric, in a nod to the "Over the Rainbow" theme, so it could billow in the wind when moved back and forth to the music. Along the front of the stick, we added the word "Love" in letters covered with rainbow feathers. The heart was covered in glow-in-the-dark paint.

But wait, there's more! (*Edit: If you didn't read that line like it was on the Price Is Right, please start again at the beginning of this guide.)* The wedding invitation said that the dress for the reception after the ceremony was "Anything Goes." Oh geez. You thought "casual elegant" was tough to dress for. What were we going to wear? It came in a vision: A few months prior, we found ourselves in Target while drunk on homemade margaritas, which were delicious but <u>not recommend</u> before entering a big box store. There, we purchased a gold lamé bikini. For the "Anything Goes" outfit, we rocked the gold top and pulled out the sewing machine to fabricate a mini skirt with some of the leftover gold lamé fabric used for the rage stick. Then we purchased a plain white mask from a craft store, drew on a third eye that had a rainbow-colored iris and covered it with rainbow feathers. Hey, they said "Anything Goes."

While wearing that wild costume, our nasty ex-boyfriend's new young girlfriend got so excited at seeing our costume and rage stick – and not recognizing who we were under it all – that she waved excitedly and pointed us out to the ex. He was, not surprisingly and quite pathetically, disgusted at our happiness and the fact that others were smiling with us. That night, our friend Stephen wore a suit covered entirely in Christmas lights that lit up, and our friend Adam created a robot costume out of boxes and dryer tubes that also lit up. It was a fantastic night.

**Above, Anything Goes**

Lots of beautiful people come together at music festivals to Make It Happen, and that means you too. The fact that you are reading this means you are IN and encouraged to do something off the wall. Consider how lovely it is when, at night in the middle of the set of one of your favorite musicians, someone in the crowd releases a glowing Chinese lantern that you can watch float far away into the clear, starry night. You can do something like this as well, making a memory for you and thousands of strangers (or, more aptly, ***future friends***.)

Once after a Dead show in Charlotte, NC, we stumbled out the wrong exit of the venue in the midst of an excited crowd. While trying to get our bearings, we walked directly past a man who was lighting fireworks off in the parking lot. We were startled.

"Hey, you should warn a sister!" the entire writing team exclaimed in unison.

The guy looked at us mischievously, winked and said under his breath, "Warning." With glee, we then proceeded to enjoy a front-row view of the rest of his awesome display.

Glowsticks are a less hazardous way to light up a crowd. Some people do not like glowsticks because, in truth, they are a bit of an environmental hazard. But they really help you feel like a kid. Look for 50-packs of glowsticks for sale at those chain drug stores during Halloween for cheap, like $5 for a tube. Buy a bunch whenever you can and ***do your future self a favor***. Do not buy those single-purchase, short green safety glow sticks. That is a different animal, and too big and pricey to throw. The "more the merrier" rule applies to glowsticks, because sometimes this activity results in a ***glowstick war***. This is something that can be found at many concerts, but especially at Phish shows.

We first saw Phish in 1995, and that was before the trend of throwing glowsticks in the air during great riffs took off. The band went on a temporary hiatus for a while, and in between we caught a band called Phix play at Langerado from 1 to 4 a.m. They played the same setlist at the same venue that Phish played with the turn of the century. The massive glowstick war – a contagious act of exuberant tossing – that ensued that night was one for the books. Ever since then, we've been pro-glow. Glowsticks, you see, are a populist way of participating. Try to throw said glowstick at a perfectly nuanced note in the song, so that the act of lobbing a piece of glowing plastic into the sky somehow adds to the performance. Throwing glowsticks during the slow, emotion-filled parts of songs is not appropriate. It's an art. Throw approximately five or six at a time, fanned out gracefully and lobbed into the air in an arch. Don't throw too low; it is not fun to be beaned in the back of the head by a glowstick. (*Edit: We are speaking from experience.*)

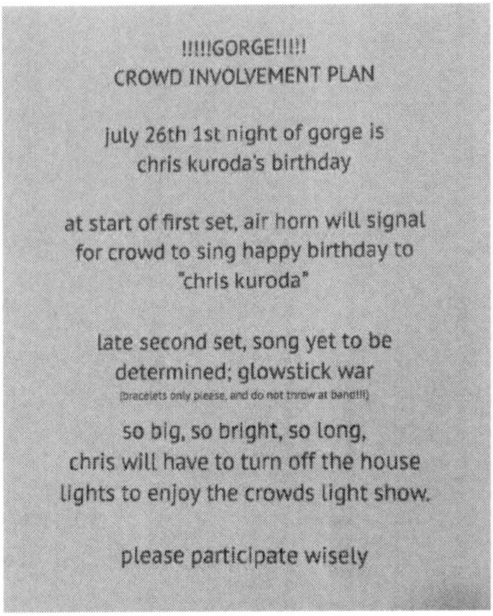

!!!!!GORGE!!!!!
CROWD INVOLVEMENT PLAN

july 26th 1st night of gorge is
chris kuroda's birthday

at start of first set, air horn will signal
for crowd to sing happy birthday to
"chris kuroda"

late second set, song yet to be
determined; glowstick war
(bracelets only please, and do not throw at band!!!)

so big, so bright, so long,
chris will have to turn off the house
lights to enjoy the crowds light show.

please participate wisely

**Left, how to organize a glowstick war**

Most hippies love glowsticks. As you know already, a glowstick can be used as excellent bait while hippie fishing. They help you feel like a little kid! Sometimes we'll collect a bunch of glowsticks from the ground. (*Edit: Don't worry, Mom, we follow the Golden Rule, which is ... come on, short term memory! ... sigh. You totally forgot didn't you. It's Don't Put Your Hands In Your Mouth. So, if you get a little dirt under your nails while picking up a previously tossed glowstick, well, no problem mon.*) Keep the fun going!

You know what crazy Jack Nicholson says in "The Shining": "All work and no play makes Jack a dull boy!" (*Edit: Insert a photo of "The Scream" here.)*

The important thing to remember when it comes to Making It Happen is the communal nature of it all. Any energy that you put into bringing smiles to your friends, your ***future friends*** and yourself is energy that is not wasted. No need to overthink this: Sometimes an inside joke is enough to inspire. Without fail at a festival, you'll see a group of friends all wearing construction outfits, with the reflective vests, hard hats and tube socks. “Safety Third!” And here they are, all laughing. It's beautiful.

Our friend and super-creative artist Scroggie and his band of ***merry pranksters*** create a Short Cut Camp every year at Spirit of the Suwannee Music Park festivals and beyond. We befriended these beautiful people because they created an experience that was really fun and engaging. Why? Because they enjoy making other people smile and meeting new friends. Mission accomplished! Our friendship started simple enough when, one festy morning over coffee, my friends asked if we had seen the Alice in Wonderland camp. It was actually right over there, they pointed, a stone's throw! What could it be?

We wandered over to discover a corridor of sheets that were painted like playing cards. Walking under an archway into the camp, we first came upon a wishing well that was built with horizontally wrapped yarn. Inside the little yarn shed, visitors were encouraged to take some confetti from a bucket and put it into the cardboard well with, of course, a wish. After that, visitors walked along the card-lined path to to discover larger-than-life, paper maché mushrooms and a mailbox, where you can write your future self a letter and they promised to mail it at an undetermined time. Next was a ***trade blanket***, where you could leave an item and take an item. Then there was the rabbit's hole, which some readers may have chosen upon entering this chapter. We were completely blown away. After climbing through the PVC pipe at the foot of the painted tree, visitors entered The Looking Glass: a groovy mirrored box that pulsed with strobed and spiraling lights. Who was behind this? We had to know. Turned out it was Scroggie. And it was his birthday!

Here's where things come full circle. See, before we left for that particular festival, our friend Danny gave us all these really beautiful, unique stones that he had collected and no longer wanted because he was moving across country. He asked us to please give them away at the festival – he helped to Make It Happen. So, we of course gave Scroggie a stone for his birthday. Then we put another stone on the trade blanket and grabbed in return a cheap, plastic cartoon-covered digital watch, which we actually needed because we had forgotten mine. ***Mind blown.***

Scroggie turned to us and said, "We are having a tea party tomorrow at 11 a.m. here at our camp. Would you like to join us?"

**Above, Short Cut Camp dressing up at the Wizard of Oz. Nailed it!**

Thanks to the trusty new watch, we arrived right on time the next day at the tea party, where everyone who was camping there had transformed into the entire cast of Alice in Wonderland. Scroggie was The Mad Hatter, of course. Megan (now Scroggie's wife and baby mama!) was Alice. Kerrie was the hookah-smoking caterpillar. Bonnie was the Cheshire cat. Kim was the Queen of Hearts. Don was the King of Hearts. Cliff is the Dormouse. These guys were really impressive! We were standing around camp, having a beer (*Edit: Did you really expect tea?),* when Scroggie said, “Hey, would anyone like to be in the jury?”

Our hand shot up. We ran back to camp and grabbed a pair of ***fairy wings*** and monster-eye headband and return in time to be given an oversized drawing pad and a marker. Here’s what transpired.

Act opens:

*Random person wearing sunglasses walks through camp with friends, looking at the playing card sheets,* ***trade blanket****, etc.*

Queen: HALT! How dare this person walk through the camp with sunglasses on while it is cloudy! OFF WITH HIS HEAD!

*Random characters cheer, echo “Off with his head! Off with his head!”*

King: Now, now dear. Wouldn’t it be best to give this person a trial?

Queen: No! OFF WITH HIS HEAD!

*Random extras cheer, king works to persuade her. He eventually succeeds. They grab the stranger by the arm and bring him over to the jury box, where we're standing.*

Everyone: A trial! A trial! A trial!

The trial included a number of "witnesses" who testified in a blow-hard manner, ending with the Dormouse, who was suddenly terrified by the Cheshire Cat. The Dormouse then ran around to the jury, knocking us down (*Edit: *Cough-cough* Not for nothing, but certain members of this writing team were leads in high school theatrical performances*).

Everyone: The jury's down! The jury's down!

As the crazy play continued, the rest of the cast all run to help us up, and then Scroggie exclaims, "And now we dance!" Everyone breaks out into a jig. And then we all laughed and let the stranger go, a little perplexed but with a story they will be telling just like we just did.

That's Making it Happen 2.0. Take a breather here; don't get overwhelmed. It is not that necessary to be so well-thought out. ***Ain't nobody got time for that***. We get it. No pressure. Sometimes <u>just being yourself allows others to be themselves as well</u>.

We remember our friend Doc. We camped with him at our very first music festival; he left an impression. Older with gray hair, he wore tie dyes and John Lennon-style, metal-framed glasses. One morning, we asked him for sugar, because we were still using sugar in our coffee at that point. He offered homemade liquid sorghum from a glass Ball jar instead. He had a copy of *The Complete Annotated Grateful Dead Lyrics* and encouraged everyone to sign on the page of their chosen song. (We chose "Sugaree" for the line: *"Just don't tell them that you know me."*)

**Left, the artist Stephen Barry ... isn't he simply glowing?**

Doc loved Dark Star Orchestra, a band that faithfully played setlists from specific Grateful Dead shows. He would simply groove out, swaying back and forth, eyes closed and just basking in good feelings. He died a few months later unexpectedly. How wonderful that he reached a point in his life when he was comfortable simply being himself.

There's no need to be ***bizarro*** if that's not who you are. By Making It Happen in your own way, you are creating the festival experience for yourself and for others who (*Edit: this may come as a shock*) might not have read this Fest Guide. By bringing joy to others, in turn you bring joy to yourself! Nothing demonstrates this more than Amanda, who we met at Jazz Fest advertising free hugs. She was carrying around a sign that read "Free Hugs" and, when you were hugged, she gave you a sticker that read – you guessed it – "Free Hugs." So suddenly you, in turn, were offering free hugs. And then everyone got a hug. Yay!

This is the ***Law of Abundance*** at its finest. For the uninitiated, this means that there is always enough of everything, all the time, for everyone. A lot of people think this is a bunch of mystical hogwash, but the entire writing team believes it. When we need money to appear for a festival ticket, it appears. When we are feeling unloved and lonely, hugs appear. Time is another example of this. Our dear friend and festy buddy Julie once commiserated with us about how our get-er-done personalities cause us to create huge to-do lists before we leave for vacation. It's as if we think we must accomplish everything in order to relax. For example, we always tidy the house before we leave. Julie raised us one: Her ex once restacked the woodpile before leaving on a vacation. Because of COURSE that couldn't wait. And yet ... we all manage to find the time to do the things that need to happen. And the things that don't get done? Funny how it all works out in the end. Letting go of the need to control and worry about the perceived lacking in life is a gift to yourself. Practice this freedom at a music festival and every day.

One way to practice this AND Make It Happen is to volunteer or work for your ticket. It can be ***easy peasy.*** Many friends will get up early to pick up litter, sort recyclables or even work with the musicians or the media in exchange for their festival pass. All of this, of course, must be set up ahead of time. If you are hoping to make it to a music festival by volunteering, start this process EARLY. Go on the web site for the festival and search out the volunteer application form. Do you know anyone who's already volunteered? Your chances for being picked for this bartering opportunity will increase through connections. DO NOT wait until the last minute for this. Just because there is abundance everywhere in the universe doesn't mean that you don't have to ***set yourself up for success***.

Highlight your skills. Our friends loved to spin fire in the backyard of their house. We'd hang out and watch them play with ***poi***. They would practice mesmerizing poi techniques all the time and were eventually able to translate these skills into tickets to music festivals. Remember JT getting burned on his shoulder because Safety Third? Now that's flow ... and Making It Happen at the same time.

Artists should always work overtime in the barter department. It's part of being creative! Would the venue enjoy some live painting during a show? How about yoga on a heavy metal cruise, like Mary did? That's all part of the gig, man.

The important part of this barter is to make sure that it works for you. Volunteering at the book tent was fun and all, but the reality was that Jazz Fest takes place from about 11 a.m. to 7 p.m. We arrived around noon and our shift at the book tent was between 1 and 4 p.m. That left just a few hours for the festival that day. Was the free ticket really worth it? Since the only band that we really wanted to see that day came on after the shift, the deal worked. If we had felt like we were missing out on something great, then it wouldn't have been a good deal. You have to figure this out for yourself. Volunteering can present another side of the festival; sometimes you are able to meet locals or new friends who are into the same things you are. I got to meet Dennis McNally. That was cool. But it's work. Just remember that.

And frankly, aren't festivals all about having fun? That's why we encourage you to save up your pretty pennies and just buy a ticket. That ex who makes bamboo lamps? Before we met, the only time he went to a music festival was to work – he called it a ***working vacation***. Depending on your finances, this could be a dream come true. But when he finally attended a festival where he didn't sell his products, he admitted that he never had so much fun. It's good to work and work hard, but it's even better to play and play hard.

**Below, the artist Bean Spence producing rad psychedelic 3D live art. He's "working."**

By buying yourself the freedom of having to answer to no one, you get to choose how you wish to spend the day. Some friends barely make it away from the camp. They enjoy eating and drinking, smoking weed and giggling. That's not us. This is when we announce: ***"There's live music happening!"*** and extract ourselves from the quicksand quagmire that often is camp. With a trusty watch on and a foldable schedule tucked into our bag, we plan our time as we see fit. We make our own ***executive decisions***. If we're not impressed with one band at one stage, we wander over to another. With a group of friends? Don't feel like you have to always ***travel as a family***. If you want to do something differently than your friends, then meet up with them later. You'll find them eventually, we promise. Doing whatever you want is a beautiful thing. Try it sometime.

Not having to "work" for your ticket during the festival proper also means that you don't have to live up to any sort of expectation or deal with anyone you don't want to deal with. One festival we were selling those bamboo lamps (*Edit: again, sigh, those damn lights*), and our neighboring vendor was a woman who is now our friend Shannon, a super-talented body painter who later went to star in a reality television show about body painters. She painted our décolleté, and it was amazing. What was less amazing was having to spend the entire rest of the day trapped in a booth working instead of enjoying the freedom that comes from being a different color. And what fun is a festival if you can't enjoy being a different color?

That all being said, clothing and costumes aren't the only thing to pack to make the scene. ***Glitter*** is a life-sustaining element of music festivals, so if you're one of those people who hate glitter, well, ***#sorrynotsorry***. There is a very good chance you will get some glitter on you at some point in the weekend. We once owned a pair of glasses with silver glittery frames that were worn at night so the lights from the stage would dance around our eyes like reflections of a disco ball. That's one way to get your glitter on without finding bits of the shiny stuff weeks later. Glitter really does get everywhere. One time we saw an ex in the crowd and sprinkled some in his hair. (*Edit: Mwhahaha*!) Have a friend incarcerated for a petty crime, like perhaps in a state where pot is still illegal? Consider sending envelopes filled with the sparkly stuff so the guards can open it and have it spill out all over their laps. You know, if you want to.

**Above, Reiki energy offerings.**

Yes, there is often a bit of a rebellious, naughty quality to Making It Happen. But it can also be sweet and loving. This writing team practices ***Reiki***, which means we offer and receive healing energy from the Universe, and sometimes we set up a blanket at a busy intersection of the festival grounds and offer free chakra balancing and aura clearing. We'll send good healing energy to people who pass and are limping (Safety Third!) or have some sort of ailment. Often, people will stop and request healing touch. One guy traded some small silver dots that are used for acupressure. He instructed us to put two of these sticky dots on different parts of our earlobes and squeeze them when we needed to either be calm or get awake. We did this many times, but never really noticed any difference.

There's an overarching theme to Making It Happen, and it's pretty simple: Be you, 100%. Be you in all your awesome glory. We never had a bigger compliment than from our friend Jasper Mosher. Jasper is a really amazing artist. He projects interesting and psychedelic displays of light and video on to the tree tops or on a side of a building, and the effect is mesmerizing. It's always a little twisted, real ***Reefer Madness*** style. People crane their necks and watch his displays for hours. In fact, we've listened to an entire Allman Bros. concert while just hanging back in the crowd and watching his art in the trees. We've also seen him create video montages on screens behind live bands, and he's really out there and a lot of fun. One night at a festival, we were watching him work and was smiling really big, when he leaned over to us.

"I've always been a fan of yours," he said. Now, we are just ourselves at a festival, no backstage passes (*Edit: yet!)* or VIP status like everyone's pal

Rex, who was voted ***Mayor of moe.down***. (*Edit: He got to wear a sash!).* Maybe that's part of Jasper's magic, that he makes people feel special. For that moment there, he sure made us feel really good. And if that's not what a music festival is all about, then we don't know what is.

Jasper, by the way, also drives a painting van around the festival grounds. You hop in the back, and there's no telling where you'll end up or when you'll get off. We have hopped on this van late at night and watch the ***spunions*** stumbling toward their campsites. Jasper drives the thing like a bat out of hell, with everyone in the back just hanging on, giggling and bouncing around. One time, when we were along for the ride, his muffler fell off, and he somehow ran it over. It was around 3 a.m. when we all piled out of the van as some guys shimmied underneath to fix it. Turns out we had broken down in the quiet family camping area. So be that a warning to you: If you think you're going to get a good night's sleep just because you're in the quiet family area, you may not. Imagine all of us crazy kids, covered in glitter and just moments ago lighting off fireworks and laughing hysterically at things like our friend pretending a random mannequin on the side of the road was his long-lost lover. Don't get mad about it. You just have to laugh along. You bought the ticket and signed up for it! Sleep is overrated anyway, yes?

# Chapter 9:
# Life On The Road

And so it goes! Mastering the Fest Life is pretty easy once you figured out Operation Big Fun. You come to appreciate the unique qualities of your brothers and sisters, enjoy the best art and food and, at the same time and certainly most importantly, jam out to some of the best live music happening today!

Going to one festival is just the beginning. Once you start Making It Happen and doing it right, you'll want to go to a lot more throughout the year. This can be tricky when juggling a full-time job and family obligations, but it's worth it. Even though Location! Location! Location! is part of the ***festy constellation***, traveling to fests is something that should be done at least a few times in your life, if only to spice things up.

We've always believed that the easiest way to find wisdom is through experience, and one way to experience the world and the many different people in it is to travel. Consider combining travel with music with a festival that isn't in your backyard.

**Left, the seat on the Merry Prankster's bus where it was Cowboy Neal at the wheel on a bus to Never Never Land.**

***It's all part of the adventure***. We've taken planes, trains and automobiles to get to the show. Which form of transport is best for you? Let's look at the different challenges for each. Planes are cool because, obviously, they will get you across the country fastest. But it's really tough to pack all the gear you need into checked baggage. A common festy trick is to immediately head to the Wal-Mart closest to the festival grounds and buy the camping gear you'll need for the weekend, only to return it a few days later, proclaiming that it was broken. (*Edit: We are not recommending this, because: legal advice.*)

Do you have friends nearby your chosen festival? Better connect with them! This is when crew can beat location in the ***festy constellation***. It's like crew is paper, and location is a rock, in other words. Always befriend the cool folks you meet along the way – they may be the key to success at another festival across the nation. Years ago, we were wandering through the crowd at Jazz Fest and met Auggie. Years later, he's working for Louie slinging Jerry rolls at festivals all over. When we were driving up to Hulaween one year, he asked us for a lift from the airport, which was on the way. No problem! We were already picking up another friend there. And while Auggie was waiting for us, he met a guy named Dustin who had the sweetest little dog. Dustin also needed a ride to the show. We strapped bags to the rack on top of the Prius, piled in and away we went. ***Happy to help!***

To travel to festivals without breaking the bank or becoming frustrated, an extended social network is crucial. We highly recommend creating a ***personal "business" card*** for yourself to give to people so you can reconnect with them after the festival. If you have a job that provides you a business card, you can certainly hand that out – you never know when your hippie friend needs a new roof, if that's what you're selling – but unlike "real life," at festivals no one really cares what you actually do for a living. At cocktail parties back home, the first question is usually, "So, what do you do?" The first question at music festivals is, "Where are you from?" Get contact information from these fine folks, and you've got yourself friends throughout the county!

Having friends in every city is a fine way to live life on the road. Driving – depending on the gas prices (that hybrid Prius really came in handy) – is a great option for seeing festivals. Many of our friends have vehicles that are specially designed for life on the road. A teardrop-shaped pull-behind camper provides a place to sleep, or adding an air mattress to the back of a station wagon can get you some shut-eye along the way. #vanlife and those tiny homes are cool trends now.

If you don't have a Transformer vehicle-turned-bed, a popular way to stay save a little cash and get some zzzz's is to ***couchsurf*** wherever you can. Here's one of our favorite jokes: How do you know a hippie crashed on your couch? He's still there!

We'd like to offer a tip of our collective writing team hats to all the wonderful friends who have let us stay with them over the years. It is a great way to experience a community while also getting to your next festival destination.

Our friends Jen and Doug let us crash at their pad every Jazz Fest, and they even give us bikes to borrow! We love biking around New Orleans, although it's not always smart with the amount of liquor that your liver is constantly processing in that city. Also, we can still feel the *woosh!* of a public bus swerving into the bike lane around the corner from the fairgrounds, nearly killing us. Ah, good times.

**Above, they're not having any fun at all.**

In exchange for the free bed and transportation, we make sure to be a cool guest. This is important, because couchsurfing is at its core an energy exchange. Always remember this. Think specifically about ways to pay back your guest. We usually do at least one ***motherload*** of dishes in the sink and stock the fridge with some local beer and yummies. And we always clean up after myself (oh, and walk the dog, too!).

Driving to festivals makes it easy to travel with the all your stuff. You might as well fill your vehicle to maximum capacity with everything you could need for the next apocalypse or music festival. Definitely pack extra food, healthy snacks especially. You may think, oh, we'll just hit a supermarket once we get there. But honestly, how many times do you want to stop by a Waffle House (to play the Waffle House theme song on the jukebox and enjoy a cup of coffee complete with a pre-applied lipstick stain and a surly waitress)? Junk food on the road gets old fast. It may seem like a good idea to get a burger at a fast food joint, but give it 30 minutes and chances are, you will regret the decision. Taco Bell in daylight hours looks a whole hell of a lot worse than Taco Bell at 2 a.m.

Also, choose your travel companions with care. Some friends we've driven long distances with are paranoid. They believe that police officers target cars with hula hoops strapped to the outside and covered in Grateful Dead stickers. Is this really true?

Possibly. We were targeted in a crowd by the cops, and we've certainly heard our share of stories about ***kynd*** folks getting pulled over and busted for drugs.

So, if your car doesn't look like a soccer mom's minivan, put the drugs away. If you have any, seriously, never leave them out in the open. EVER. If you want to use drugs, and we've certainly discussed this here as part of ***Operation Big Fun***, so we're not making some sort of moral proclamation. We're being practical: Use and immediately store.

**Right, he won the party on Jam Cruise and has the trophy to prove it.**

It's not too much of a stretch to think that a bunch of dreadlocks would garner the attention of some cops. (Edit: ***6 up***!) It's a bummer to see some heads get busted, but we doubt anyone is really in shock that the Volkswagen Vanagon covered in stickers got pulled over. The reality is that hippies are profiled by cops second only to every minority nowadays. Talk to some old timers, and they'll tell stories about getting stopped in some po-dunk town in the backwoods of the Deep South. Right out of Central Casting is the cop, spitting some tobacc-y, and breaking a headlight with their billy club to provide reason for the stop. Man, all we want is a little peace and love!

So be smart about it. Regardless of the kind, always <u>blow smoke directly out the window</u> – no ***hotboxing*** – and put everything away that you don't want to be seen. Of course, any cop worth his or her salt will still rummage ... which brings us back to security.

We've talked a lot about how to beat the system of the security guards and not let them kill your buzz, both figuratively and literally. On the road, security takes on a whole new meaning. When you travel from festival to festival, even if there is a stop for a little work in between, you start to become a part of the counterculture. There's no other way to describe it. It is definitely an alternative universe, being a hippie and going to these festivals. You probably already know this, but it should be discussed directly. We're not big on the whole "us v. them" scenario, but there are a lot of people who do feel that way. We do enjoy the sight of a hippie successfully running from a security guard, and no one likes their festy friends getting busted by the police. We don't want you to be one of those people. Know your rights.

We know a few great lawyers who go to shows and are helpful when it comes to helping hippies when there is the possibility of arrest. But the best advice, which we think would be remiss if absent, is to not get caught in the first place. Be smart. Remember that story about the undercover cop with the weed pipe? Yeah. Sometimes they try to trap you, but other times these police officers are just doing their job. So, don't speed. Don't have billows of smoke coming out your window. Don't blast music at intersections – all that obvious stuff that causes beautiful people to go through serious and expensive hassles. It's a fine line, Making It Happen while not being a dumb ass. Whether it's the police or a security guard, whether they're super-lame and uptight or cool, remember that they do have authority so ***be cool, fool***.

One thing some festy folks do that will certainly call unnecessary attention on the road is leaving on their wristbands. It's great to go to a bunch of festivals and a fun souvenir to keep a wrist-load of tickets. These wristbands are usually colorful and cloth, so you can wash with them and they're going to last. For some people, cutting off the wristband is a painful reminder that it is time to return to "the real world." But do it. This writing team is like a pack of wild animals leaving a zoo at the end and, if wild animals had access to scissors or opposable thumbs, we cut that thing almost immediately. But other people are different and want to keep it as a souvenir. So, here's how to save your memento while not calling unwanted attention to your hippie self.

How to remove one of those cloth wristbands without cutting: (*Edit: This is also important information for those times when the person at the ticket booth is mindless or malicious and puts your wristband on too tight for your liking.)* The thing with these types of wristbands, as festival veterans know, is that they can become tighter but they cannot become looser. This is obviously so that it's "impossible" to share wristbands. This trick can also help friends economically and fraudulently, if so inclined. To remove or loosen the wristband, grasp the circular plastic piece that tightens the band. In your other hand, twist the two ends of the wristband until it becomes one, tight piece. In the opposite direction from your twist, turn the plastic connector thing toward the ends of the wristband. Be methodical and intentional in your twisting, and you will be able to loosen said wristband. My buddy Haps taught me that trick. You're welcome.

On the flipside of all that are the high rollers. Are you a high roller? (*Edit: If this is the case, could you buy a bunch of these Fest Life Guides and give them to all your friends as gifts? Thank you!)* High rollers, or those who like to live large, splurge on ***VIP***. In general, people who pay VIP are less likely to cruise around and go to a bunch of festivals. That can get pretty expensive. Our guess is that people who pay extra for VIP usually just go to one festival and feel like big shit. They kind of are! We've personally never purchased a VIP package, because we simply enjoy the art of being crafty and frugal and not in debt. But many, many people buy VIP tickets. Besides a much higher price tag, VIP tickets usually include a special section to sit that's usually pretty close to the stage. Some festivals reserve the first 10 yards, at least, for VIP. Other festivals will reserve a section to one side of the stage. VIP-ers often get cleaner bathrooms (nice perk!) and sometimes get food and drink included. It totally depends on the deal. We would say it is not worth it in the end, but others may disagree.

Our understanding of the VIP ticket is that it's simply an up-sell for those who want luxury in a venue that is anything but. Hey ***Mr. Money Bags***, go big. You can get a luxury RV with air conditioning and showers for festivals, of course. Have meals catered or bring amazing feasts like smoking an entire hog or whatever excites you gastronomically. By all means, do NOT deal with the riff-raff. We don't know if VIP-ers get fewer things stolen or have any better of a time, really. Try it and report back.

There are two important pieces of advice for those who plan on VIP: First, take advantage of every cool thing you possibly can! ***Ride the rail*** if that's the benefit, or eat and drink like the pig that some are roasting. Get your money's worth. (This goes for motels and hotels that you must stay in along the way, if you are going to a festival and don't have friends en route. Hit the pool! Get some ice! Just beware of that mini bar ....) Secondly, and even more importantly, don't let your expensive ticket stop you from making friends. No need to feel better than anyone just because you've got a couple bucks burning a hole in your pocket.

**Right, we're gonna take a guess here that maybe Oscar isn't VIP. Note, these are grown men. Haters, scram!**

Making new friends is just the very best part of the festival experience, second only to witnessing amazing musical history that only comes from live performances. Don't miss out! It's easy as an adult to just sort of hang out with the friends you came with, because, frankly, it's so very fun to share laughs and music with your friends. Don't get us wrong here; We're not suggesting you not sit around the campfire and have a wonderful time with your friends. Just do not be too shy to make new ones!

Many adults forget how to make friends. Lots of adults confuse the mating process with making friends. But, news flash: Not everyone you talk to has to be someone you want to have sex with. That's such a common reason, especially for those who are single or those who come to a festival and plan on cheating or just pretending to be single. Making friends with someone doesn't have to be about that. You can simply be a nice person who is genuinely curious and interested in the different opinions and perspectives of the people around you. Expand your horizons.

Festivals are ideal for this! Usually, you travel to a music festival primarily because you love the music. And guess what? So does (most) everyone else! It's like everyone around you has been vetted in some way so they're a potential friend. You have one thing in common with everyone else at the festival! It's easy to spark new friendships. Need a refresher for friend-making as an adult? It's really simple:

Step 1: Smile. Reach out your hand to the person.

Step 2: Say, "Hi! My name is ______. What is your name?"

Step 3: Look them in the eye pleasantly.

Step 4: Give them a good handshake.

**Above, more of the *framily* including Peter, Denise, Kristina, Lee, Jeff and Patrick looking toasty at SunFest.**

Now, a lovely reality of festivals is that quite often someone will ***prefer to hug***. We do both. We like to look people in the eye before we embrace them. It puts everyone on an equal playing field. This writing team, collectively, is a pretty good read of character – it's one of our strengths, if we do say so ourselves – so we like the opportunity to see if someone is shifty-eyed. Not everyone is a good person, we hate to tell you. Always use and ***trust your instinct*** about the people around you. Some people will steal, lie or do you wrong in a variety of ways. Look, we're don't think you're stupid. It's just that the magic utopian qualities of music festivals can delude ***kynd*** folks into thinking that just because you are in the same scene as someone else means that they are a fair, loyal, honest and trustworthy individual. That's not always the case.

Let's take a moment here to get back to basics. If you are single and have taken the Fest Life on the road, you will eventually ***hook up*** with someone at a music festival. In fact, many people will go to music festivals just to get a little sexual action. It's part of adult life, so we might as well address this.

We know a guy in the music festival scene who is simply not attractive. By no stretch of any imagination would this weathered-looking guy with a beer belly and gray hair turn any head, ever. We won't name him because it's not nice but it's the truth and so for purposes of this guide, you can simply imagine an ugly man. BUT! He has an endless stream of ladies by his side who just fall madly in love with him. We've seen it time and time again. What is his magic? Music, obviously.

This guy is a really great musician. He's really talented, and lots of people enjoy seeing and hearing him play. We do not deny that he is a talented and skilled musician and an OK nice guy. But what we cannot get behind is the sheer number of women who are blinded by it.

Long before disco divas were "making eyes across the dance floor" with some dude in a leisure suit, people were hooking up with unsavory characters. It is extremely common, and frankly quite easy, at a music festival. This is why we highly caution against this activity.

Sure, there are many stories of people finding the love of their lives at music festivals, and that's awesome. But those couples are the exception. The norm is one-night-stands or relationships that last as long as the festival and then the potential for hurt feelings. (*Edit: Or worse! Use protection always! Pack condoms, people.*) Sex takes away from the most important things at a festival, which is, of course, music. Many people may live in small towns and have problems finding potential mates, but really go into this experience with your eyes opened to what it is. If you are cool with a casual fling, and you are careful to use protection so your temporary fun doesn't have lingering effects on the rest of your life, then have at it. We're not judging. We just are so tired of hearing about our girlfriends who are super-heartbroken over that troll of a dude who's so vain, he probably thinks this paragraph is about him.

There are many different types of people to meet at a music festival. It's a little like going into a kava bar. At every kava bar we've ever been to, it's like every kind of pot smoker walks through the door: the b-boys, the hippies and the artists ... these people are generally creative types. That's worth noting, too: Be inspired by different people around you. Do not presume that everyone is an enemy, and don't presume that everyone wants to have sex. <u>Find a friend in everyone</u> – a real friend. But trust your gut if your instinct tells you otherwise. That's an important rule of the road.

This circles back to safety. If someone creeps you out, don't be around them. Leave. Never, ever purchase anything from someone who creeps you out. Some folks who travel to festivals are looking for items that are sold by those who whisper words under their breath as you are walking past them on ***Shakedown Street***, or they come around to campsites. This is often a wonderful capitalist scenario, having these sellers come to you. Whether it's homemade ***lot shirts***, psychedelic drawings or chocolate mushrooms, it's worth talking to the person. Admire their art. Find out where they are camping and how long they've been coming to the festival. If you are at all receptive, you'll get a feeling for who these people are. That's when you know whether to support them or not. We once bought a bubble wand from a hippie in the crowd of Jazz Fest. What a sweet guy.

The bubble wand was metal with amethysts and wire twisted into heart shapes. He was blessing the crowd with bubbles, and, well, you know, "***Bubble Girl***!" We wanted one. But really what we wanted to do was honor this guy and his art. That's really what commerce is about, isn't it? While you are traveling, if you can, purchase things from people who are clearly good-hearted and creative. This is positive karma, helping people on their path toward good.

**Left, Bubble Girl, Native American incarnation (our apologies to any bubble-hating Native peoples) as captured by SeeBliss Photography at the Orange Blossom Jamboree**

Conversely, in general, people with low vibrations sell you bad stuff. The trick is to recognize your ***buying power*** with vendors of all types and spread the love. Festivals are also vacations. Souvenirs are a good idea!

Of course, back to the priority of what festivals are all about: Our favorite souvenir is a CD of a band we've just discovered at the festival. Play that on the ride home and smile at the amazing, life-changing, glorious weekend you just had!

# Epilogue

Are you ready now? We are hopeful that by reading this guide, you'll be the most prepared and happy person at the festival. You'll be the one who will make people smile. You will have the best time ever, without any drama or worry, because you've already taken care of everything. You'll be wise and help others. You'll be the one people turn to, but not so much that it's kind of annoying because hey man, you're here to have a good time! With the information in this manual, you'll be able to rock out the festival and return to your "normal" life at home, feeling healthy, with a big smile and lots of beautiful memories. Congratulations on enjoying the best live music scenes happening right now! Now ***let's rage***!

OK ... so did you rage already? It was super-rad, wasn't it? Just like this book, yes? Would you write a review for it on Amazon? Thanks ***framily***!

## The Fest Life Glossary

Speak the language, people. Get with the program.

### *A*

***Ain't nobody got time for that*** If you do not know this reference, please search online for the "Sweet Brown AutoTune Remix" and enjoy. Then watch the "Bed Intruder" video. Timeless.

### *B*

***because, hippies*** Sometimes, there is no explanation for why this group of groovy folks refuse to follow along with rules and norms. It just is, so you best get used to it.

***big picture safety*** Safety means a lot of things. It means not breaking a bone, not poisoning yourself, not getting arrested, not endangering others and definitely not saying yes when some dude in the Grateful Dead lot has a cool-looking, lime green school bus and offers to "give you a tour of the inside and let you sign your name on the wall."

***bizarro*** Weird, crazy, fabulous. Stick a googly-eye with a rainbow-colored iris on your third eye, grab a Rasta pasta and split, *Señor Bizarro Montebon*.

***be cool, fool*** Mr. T's excellent advice that applies to almost every situation.

***bubble girl*** We did not realize that this was a thing until we invested $1 into a bubble wand, then suddenly people would say aloud, "Oh, look, there's the bubble girl" as if there was only one person in the entire festival who had the forethought and discretionary budget to buy a bubble wand. Granted, sometimes we were the only one at a concert blowing bubbles, but this does not make us hang our entire identity on this toy.

***The Bundle Bandit*** A veddy, veddy bad man. This man took his toys and WENT HOME! (Edit: *Booo!*) *See also:* ***don't be a jerk***

***buying power*** The power of the coin! When you have a couple bucks in your pocket, you have the power to support the right kind of people selling the right kind of product. What does that mean? It means being honest, responsible, original, high quality. The people who should receive your cash are those who care about what they're selling. You have the power to support people like this, and in turn you have the power to make more people like this in the world. That's pretty awesome, financially and energetically.

## *C*

***camp landmarks*** By letting your freak flag fly, literally, you help create a sense of place in a campground. It's a smart move to mark the boundaries of your camp within seconds of arrival, before you pop your tent or crack that first beer. Get creative: lights strung in trees, big tapestries, hand-painted signs, lawn ornaments, carved pumpkins ... the crazier the better. However, don't spend a lot of money on landmarks, as they have been known to disappear. And you really don't want to know what Kenny did with that mannequin at Orange Blossom Jamboree late at night. Trust us.

***Camp Where's My ...?*** Hey, has anyone seen our aluminum foil? We know we packed those tapestries. Yeah, we've got an extra propane thing somewhere around here. We KNOW we brought a nail file! Did we really forget the can opener? Ugh, where is that warm knit cap? Where's our toothpaste, dish soap, ketchup, glitter, afro wig, glow sticks, pogo stick?

***(Bring) Coffee*** Yes, there is almost always a stand that will sell coffee, but camp coffee is the best! Not only will it keep you regular, but it is exactly that slap-across-the-face you need to face another day of insanity. Pro tip: Bring Bailey's Irish Cream.

***Constant vigilance*** That divot in the field? Watch out. That glowstick coming right at your eye? Watch out. Someone coming through the crowd somehow holding five full beers? Watch out. You must be on guard at all times. Always notice what's around you. We're not suggesting paranoia; we're suggesting you be ready for whatever is coming at you. *See also:* ***6 Up***

***cooler etiquette*** This includes, but is not limited to: opening the cooler as little as possible as to not melt the ice, wrapping all food items securely as to not seep into other foods, keep foods covered with ice as much as possible, purchasing ice for a friend if you know he or she is running low and ensuring the lid is properly closed. It's basically be respectful. Is that so hard?

***cooler failure*** Oh geez. It's such a bummer. Maybe cooler water leaked into your ***fixins***. Maybe the lid breaks off and it won't seal. Maybe that dude who's a friend of a friend doesn't wrap his meat right and it ruins all the vegetarian food you brought. There are many potentials; don't let it happen to you.

***couchsurf*** We've slept on so many couches over the years, but only in the last couple months signed up for that app. Overall, it is to stay with friends along the way. It's a lot of fun and you already know they're not going to murder you in your sleep. (*Edit: Way to jinx)*

***couch-tour*** Technology at its finest, this is when some admirable person in the crowd (or perhaps the venue themselves) will – clandestine or not – tape the concert

and stream it live over the interwebs. When the cosmic stars do not quite align and you are unable to attend a festival featuring a musical act you love, couch tour is the next best thing. For some, couch tour is even better, what with the craft beers in the frig, clean bathroom and comfortable bed every night. But don't get lazy, people. There are experiences to be had outside the living room.
***cupcakes*** We once made vegan applesauce cupcakes for our friends' festival wedding because they did not need refrigeration but were super-moist and yummy. Then we gave the big Tupperware containers that we had to buy to store said cupcakes as a present to the newlyweds, because who doesn't need Tupperware. Surely not you. See also, ***perma-grin***

## *D*

***day bags*** Do you think this writing guide is encouraging you to pack the kitchen sink? It may feel that way, but we don't want your friends to laugh at your diva ways. Instead, we want to make sure you can carry your stuff for the day comfortably through security without hassle. Bring a small backpack and a cloth grocery bag at the least. If you don't use it, chances are a friend will be in need of a loaner.
***Dead lot*** The term "lot" is simply the parking lot. Dead lot is a broad term that defines the mini-community that springs up when our favorite heady bands come to town. *See* ***dirtheads*** *... speaking of:* If they don't believe in shampoo, what DO they believe in? That vaccines cause adultism? Doubt it. These guys (there are some women in this collective, but fewer) don't give a funk. As a result, they will probably try to steal your things. Beware.

***Dirty Hippy*** A hot soy chai latte with two shots of espresso. Order it with peace fingers up, baby.
***distraction*** A hippie's best friend against security. It doesn't always work, but it's worth a try because isn't it fun to sneak things in through security (*Edit: bombs and other items that could injure others excluded)? See also:* ***Shakedown Street***
***doing your future self a favor*** Examples include: tidying your bed so you can fall right on in, brushing your hair so you don't have a baby dreadlock forming in the back, eating something before the show so you're not hungry, bringing in an unopened bottle of water through the security gates, remembering that sweatshirt, purchasing a 50-pack of glowsticks when they are on sale a couple months before festival season, etc. *See also:* ***long-term thinker***
***donkey dicking*** One of the writing team's string of former lovers used this line. WTF? It basically means to drag your feet. Is this referencing that donkeys have big penises? Conveniently, this is not a family guide. Oh. Did we forget to mention this is rated a solid PG-13? Anyway, yeah, this isn't a phrase we really recommend using in pleasant company, but it's worth knowing what other people are saying. Especially if you plan on living with this person for three years before waking up one day and saying, honestly, writing team, WTF.
***don't be a jerk*** There can only be so many Golden Rules in this guide, because it's only a guide and not a rule book, per se, but this is just a life lesson for ya. The cooler you are, the fewer problems you will have. This is especially true in crowds. Relax, mon! There is no need to cause problems.

## *E*

***e*** the most impressive and modern of the letters, although in reality we like the letter 'z' better but don't tell e

***easy peasy*** La la la! (*Edit: Get back to work!)*

***executive decisions*** Do we want a second veggie burger? Hold on, we need to consult our team. OK, no, thank you. We are plenty full. Executive decisions are one of the joys of being an adult. You get to decide things for yourself. Your mommy isn't going to be there to tell you what to do. You get to take control of your life by making the best decision you can muster at the time. Congratulations, you are an executive. You are executing your life.

## *F*

***fairy wings*** For ladies especially, fairy wings are a wonderful addition to any festival experience. Here's the thing: Do not buy large ones. They will make it difficult to enter and exit a bathroom stall or, God forbid, a Port-O-John. Fairy wings also are known to break and result in a frowny face, so just be prepared for that potentiality. However, these glittery wings attach to shoulders with small pieces of elastic and will help you remember what an angelic creature you really are, sister.

***festy constellation*** The holy triumvirate of: excellent line-up, awesome venue and free-wheeling friends ready to play. Keep in mind, this is also a bit of a shell game, because sometimes if you have the right crew, you can make it happen in a location that may at first seem really wrong for you.

***festy fashions*** Your grooviest, most colorful, more comfortable, fun, smile-inducing party clothes! Nothing that doesn't make you want to dance, twirl, be warm or cool (depending), encourage you to grab a hula hoop or a drink. *See also:* ***party pants***

***festival feet*** Oh, God. We don't even want to talk about it, let alone think about it! Gah! Have you SEEN those feet!? Let alone smell them. Open-toed shoes result in festival feet. Walking in those comfy shoes that make your feet stink? Festy feet as well. It can be very, very bad. Veddy veddy bad. We feel bad just writing this glossary section. Oh, geez. There are some things you simply cannot unsee! (*Edit: Editors are paid the big bucks due to their iron guts. To address festival feet, frequently use a wet wipe on your feet. It is smartest to make this cleaning the last phase of your body, because you will want to throw away anything that touches festival feet.)* Every once in a while, we'll see someone receiving a foot massage. Now that's love. *See also:* ***gnarsty***

***festival find*** Different than a ***ground score***, a festival find is the discovery of a new and favorite band. Always plan on checking out at least one new act; never stick to simply the tried and true. Getting in the know regarding new and fantastic music is a major reason to get yourself to a festival.

***festy foodies*** You know these types: They see someone selling empanadas on the side of the road and get really excited. Or you ask them what's in the cooler and they talk about marinating their pork loin or something crazy. These people LOVE FOOD. Hey, whatever gets you excited ... just so it's second to the music.

***first light early birds*** A description of time of very late night/very early morning, when you've been up all night, having a most excellent time, and suddenly you recognize something on the far horizon that looks like the first glimpse of sunlight. Stop for a moment and listen. Are those the first birds waking up? THIS IS THE TIME TO GO TO SLEEP! Make a decision to rest for a few hours at this point is the smartest thing you can do. *See also:* ***doing your future self a favor, FOMO*** *and* ***spunions***

***fixin's*** If you want to throw a couple frozen veggie burgers in your cooler for an evening meal (highly encouraged), why not also get a little baggie and fill it up with sliced pickles, lettuce, a tomato (slice this later at camp), some onion and even jalapenos! Suddenly that burger is restaurant quality, and all it took was five minutes preparing in your kitchen a few days prior. Don't worry if you've forgotten the condiments. See glossary entry above; your neighbors will definitely let you have a squirt of ketchup.

***FOMO*** Fear Of Missing Out, we think it's going to be listed in the DSM-5 as a new psychological condition, partial to millennials.

***Food is the fuel*** Yes, yes, that was a delicious burger. But what was really great about it is that it fueled you up for an evening of running around. Remember this when a bag of Doritos is in front of you – what will it take to keep you going all day and all night? This is what food is at a music festival. What feels great in the belly but won't weigh you down? (*Edit: No one wants to be around someone who is farty in a crowd, either!)*

***framily*** Are you a black sheep in your biological family? Do they think you're "a little crazy"? Have you been labeled an "indigo child"? Well, come on in for a big hug, baby, because you're part of our framily! That's right, friends are family, and we really, really love you. *If you're a Phish head, see also:* ***phamily***

***freaker by the speaker*** A Keller Williams allusion referring to a fan who wants to be in the front but can't quite find space in the center of the crowd so they linger toward the clearer outer edges. Why are there so few people in these outer edges? Because the speakers are BLASTING so that the fine folks who are 100 yards away can still hear the music. It's all well and good to dance, but not at the long-term expense of your hearing. The writing team of The Fest Life Guide do not recommend you do this.

***Fresh Sesh*** *See also:* ***hippie shower***

***freakazoid*** Oh geez, may you never really know the true meaning of this word. These are people who are just weird. Maybe they dance really close to you at a concert, and you turn away toward your friends and then suddenly there he is again, not getting the f-ing hint. Or maybe she engages you in a very long-winded conversation in the bathroom line, and then continues WHILE you are in the stall. They are on the verge of, or actively are, freaking out. *See also:* ***Bundle Bandit***

***future friends*** Who ARE these people? If you do not know someone, it is preferable to consider them a future friend rather than as stranger. Imagine how road rage will dissipate if you simply remember that these fellow drivers are not obstacles in your life, but your neighbors. Everyone is a future friend. Ain't life grand?

## *G*

***G.A.*** General Admission. This means, no chairs unless you bring it in and try to claim your stake with the chair. We will warn you: Hippies will step over your chair. They will sit in your chair when you go to the bathroom or whatever. People don't really respect chairs, so bring one if you want but don't get mad if someone is pushing through your chair because you are blocking the path that is just 10 feet from their friends. You can stake your claim with a blanket, too, but people will step on the blanket. Chill out. One time we walked through the crowd and someone on a blanket said, "Excuse me, you are walking through our living room!" We pretended to wipe our feet and continued on.

***get it while the gettin's good*** Like the rest of your life, you must snatch opportunities while you can. Is there an open Port-0-John and everyone is spacing out? Grab it. Is someone selling neat handcrafted Steal-Your-Face coasters at the campsite? Buy 'em. (*Edit: "Hey, there's a little mac and cheese left. Anyone hungry?")* Do not wait to be left in the dust, friends. Like Janis Joplin sang, "Get it while you can!"

***glitter*** A little sparkly magic goes a long way. In fact, chances are you will discover some glitter on your person weeks after the festival, and it will probably make you smile.

***glowstick war*** It's a good thing (in our opinion). Yes, yes, music is the priority and for some, when fellow festivalgoers throw glowsticks into the air excitedly during certain parts of a song (this is sometimes planned in advance, via the interwebs), it can be distracting. However, talk about a fun scene! Start with the 50-pack you picked up for cheap, and remove all the excess packaging before heading through security. This will mean less trash for volunteers to pick up. Next, crack 'em and shake the glowsticks to get them glowing. Then wait for awesome parts of the show when you can throw five or six in a pretty fan-like pattern in a high arch in the air. Once your supply is gone, you can go back to dancing or rummage around on the ground to collect another bunch for a perfectly timed toss.

***gnarsty*** *See also:* ***festival feet***

***go time*** Little Johnny raises his hand. "Yes, Johnny?" Little Johnny looks uncomfortable, shifts from side to side and looks around him. "I gotta go," he says. "I gotta GO!" OK, Johnny. It's go time. *See also **"There's live music happening"** and **Just sayin'***

***Go to your happy place*** What must be done in any Port-O-John situation. OK, let's take a moment to create our happy places, shall we? Close your eyes, which is an interesting request for a written guide. Where were you most happy? On a beach, in the sun, with a piña colada in your hand, your lover next to you, glistening from a frolic in the waves and smiling a big, toothy grin? Or are you hiking up a rocky path? Look, there's the crest! Two more steps and: Wow. What a vista! (Wait! Don't breathe in too deeply! You're really in a Port-O-John. And your business here is done, get the hell OUT!)

***Golden Rule of Festival Crowds**:* Talkers in the back! This also applies to video takers and picture takers. Look, scoot up to the front, snap a great pic and then get back to your spot. Don't stand front and center and hold up your iPhone. You are not a journalist. Simply enjoy the music. The middle of a crowd listening to great music is not the time to tell your friend about that one time when ... Seriously. *See also **STFU***

***Golden Rule of Fest Health*:** Don't put your hands in your mouth! You don't know where they've been.

***Good vibes only*** It's a pretty simple way to make friends and, in turn, ***framily***. What does this mean, exactly? We guess it's more of a feeling, but good vibes aren't fighting, complaining, worrying, being paranoid, being low-vibrational in any way. Good vibes are encouraging, helpful, loving and attractive.

***grately*** Tee-hee! This is a punny way to write "greatly." *See also,* ***heads***
***ground score*** When you find something cool on the ground that's been dropped by a fellow festival fan. There are endless examples of ground scores, but by far the best is money. It's a fine line, though – don't look down at the ground all the time! A Rastafarian once told us to look up at the beautiful day. Right on, Rastamon. Make sure that when claiming a ground score that it is, in fact, abandoned property. Be honest here. Look around and really be sure that no one is running back for their thing that you found. If you think it's someone's, ask them. Be cool. Don't go stealing stuff. Also, worth repeating: Do not ingest drugs you find on the ground, ever.
***grugly*** Mix of grumpy and ugly. *No bueno.*

## *H*

***Happy to help!*** Say this often. It's good for the soul.
***heads*** Fans who let the music go straight to their heads, man! Deadheads, Phishheads, rolly polly fish heads. "Heady" music is psychedelic in nature, which mean that it inspires you to do more than simply snap your fingers and tap your toes. Heads wear tie-dye, slap Steal Your Face stickers on their vehicles and get really excited when you say simply things like, "Oh, you like the Grateful Dead? Me too." *See* ***wookie*** *although remember Don Henley saw a Deadhead sticker on a Cadillac (Edit: You can never go back, don't you ever go back.)*
***hells to the no*** We said NO! Double-snap, bitches!
***Hippie bathday!*** *Enjoy it, as it only comes once a year.* Isn't this a funny way to wish someone a happy birthday? *See also:* ***heads***

***hippie shower*** Described in length in Chapter 2. Basically, this is the process one undergoes when they're in a rush, don't have running water but need to freshen up and also happen to be camping outdoors and running around like a crazy person from one stage to the next, hugging scores of friends and sweating while dancing. But if a friend sees you, and you've got your hair combed, sporting a fresh set of clothes, teeth brushed, smelling of a wondrous mix of deodorant and patchouli, you've likely just had your hippie shower. *See also:* ***long-term thinker***
***hippie on the run*** Seen frequently in the VIP section that a hippie was able to smuggle themselves into, the "hippie on the run" is, simply, a true cliché. Mostly young lanky males, often carrying a backpack that gets thrown to the side during the chase. Because, of course, these fine folks are probably getting chased by the security guard or the cops. Most of the time, our money's on the hippie. These guys can book it!
***hippie fishing*** A very fun game that usually involves a thin and long piece of string attached to an item that would be attractive to a hippie. Bait includes: a dollar bill, a neon glow stick, a clean-looking sandwich ... use your creativity. Set the trap and wait for someone to try to pick up your item, then gently pull it away before they can get it. Laughs are guaranteed to ensue.
***hook up*** Is this like, like you like you? Or just like you? Hooking up is the general term for coupling in some fashion. It may not mean "go all the way," but really that's probably what it means. It can also mean, simply, connecting near Louie's ***Jerry Roll*** and falafel stand at a specific time so you can walk into the crowd with your friend. But this is the most common way of expressing an often-casual sexual encounter.

***hotboxing*** This is a very unadvisable habit of some people who roll up the windows in a vehicle and smoke weed. This is done because they don't want to attract attention with the fragrance of their federally illegal herb, and an added benefit is a "contact high" that can result through second-hand smoke. This is a bad habit. Your vehicle will smell like weed, your clothes will smell like weed; you'll be high and stinky. If you're worried about getting arrested, this is a very bad combination.

## *I*

***If you're having fun, you're doing it right***. A great and debatable mantra. One time we were wasting our time, not writing this glossary and instead on Facebook discussing the merits of having a bread machine, which is bigger than a bread box '*mkay*, on a forum of women who live on sailboats, because that's exactly what we did for a couple years after a long haul of festing. We wrote that taking up all that space and energy when you can make seriously awesome homemade bread in your little oven on the boat was "doing it wrong." And whoa doggie! Those ladies were super-pissed! God forbid you tell someone they're doing it wrong, when they're obviously doing it wrong. What kind of retired rich lady on a yacht in the Bahamas doesn't have time to knead bread for 15 minutes? Do you know what a pain it is to keep the batteries charged on a sailboat, and you want to plug in a bread maker? Next you'll want a hairdryer! There are consequences to life, that's all what we're talking about. Anyhoo, there's a right and a wrong, and the writers of this guide have it down, as far as we're concerned. But what if you're having fun killing people, you ask? What THEN, guide writing team? HMM! Oh, silly editor in our heads. You are starting to understand the definition of fun that can be found by doing it right at a music festival.

***Introduce yourself to those around you*** Making friends is actually as easy as, "Hi, my name is _______." What is your name? I'm excited to see this live music! Would you like a piece of gum?"

***It's all part of the adventure*** Related is the phrase "It's a process." This is a very good mantra when things are not going as you expected. Our friend John once told us that it's not really an adventure until you're a little afraid. That's solid.

## *J*

***Jerry roll*** If you've ever seen Jerry Garcia, you have also heard that guy in the crowd yelling, "Jerrrraaaaayyy!" Well, Falafel Louie has memorialized "that guy" with his delicious Jerry rolls, which are an institution at every festival we've ever attended throughout the nation. Jerry rolls are like big egg rolls. To be honest, we like his falafel best.

***Just sayin'*** What!? We're just sayin'.

## *K*

***kynd*** Even though this is a guidebook, we are unsure of the origins of why the word "kind" is spelled with a "y" instead of an i. We presume it has to do with the alternative nature of the community in which it arose, much like feminists spelling it "womyn" But mostly say this word because it is a name for a really great weed. It's beyond meaning "420-friendly;" to be kind, you must be gentle, peaceful, caring and generally cool.

# L

***Law of Abundance*** Let us save you a little time: This is "The Secret." If you believe that there is enough money, time, love, energy ... you name it ... to go around, then, news flash! There is! All you have to do is have faith, and all will come to you. Of course, you'll never just sit on the couch with your hand down your pants waiting for a paycheck. You need to participate in life in order to reap the benefits of the energy exchange. You must seek what you want without buying into the fear that "there won't be enough." There will always be enough. Really!

***Leave no trace*** Any backpacking enthusiast has heard this term before. It means you should leave the area you are in as good or better shape than you found it. That means pick up your trash. Crush that empty water bottle and put it in your pocket. Bag all your trash from your campsite and put it in the dumpster or trash can. Come on. Don't be a slob.

***let's rage*** Loosely translated as, "Now let's go have a wonderful, safe, fun time listening to music we love, OK?" *See also:* ***rage stick***

***limin*** This is a threshold we walk through throughout life. Think back to the last big crossroads in your life: maybe it was when you realized it was time to quit your job, move to a new town, when you first saw the person you're dating, when you got that cool offer. These are important experiences in our lives that transcend space and time. When you enter a limin, or a crossroads, you must make an *executive decision*. Blue pill or red pill? It's destiny, baby. Dig it.

***long-term thinker*** Crucial characteristic of an evolved person. This comes with maturity but also practice.

Thinking long term and not short term will help you remain self-sufficient and, we think, overall happier. I mean, we are always thinking short term: What do you want for a snack? Put on the blinker, time to turn right. Is that an itch? Scratch it. But what about anticipating your own needs and those of others? Now you've got it. See also ***do your future self a favor***

***Look at the schedule when planning meals*** When packing food for a festival, the most important thing is ... you guessed it ... music. So when is your favorite bands playing? Will you only have time to grab a takeaway in between sets, or can you scoot back to camp and whip up a sandwich real quick? Is there one day when all your friends want to have a group meal? Figure out the best time so it's not overlapping live music.

***looky-loos*** These festivalgoers will look at handmade art and crafts and say aloud, "I could make that." They will take pictures of the crafts instead of buying one. They are proverbially kicking tires.

***lot shirts*** When it comes to "***merch***," or merchandise that is sold officially by the band at that tent kinda near the stage for, on average $30+ per shirt, sometimes it sucks. I mean, simply bad design. An alternative is sold by some kid walking around with a bulging backpack filled with shirts he and his buddy made. These are known as lot shirts, and they're not as good of screen-printing quality, as the official merch, no doubt. But sometimes they're extra-rad, with tie-dye or funny sayings. Sometimes, bands crack down on lot shirts because the random hippie used their logo to make a buck. *Thus, see also:* ***hippie on the run***

***love*** Is it all you need? Well, geez. You sure wasted your time reading this guide, didn't you. Conveniently, love is the answer to most all problems. So we know you still love us.

## M

***making the scene*** Not to be confused with "making A scene." When we say "scene," we mean, of course, the entire festival experience. But this is true wherever you go. If you walk into a bar and you're all frowny face, you'll probably be in a lame, sad bar. If you walk in like a rainbow tornado and are all smiles, chances are others are going to respond with smiles too. You get to decide; you have a responsibility to make your life fun and amazing. *See:* ***you make it happen***

***Mango Freezes*** This is a mango smoothie sold by WWOZ as a fundraiser at Jazz Fest in New Orleans. Not only should you only listen to WWOZ while you are in NOLA, you should also buy mango freezes at Jazz Fest. Add smuggled-in rum if you know what's up.

***Mayor of moe.down*** It will always be Rex to us. Long live Rex!

***merch tent*** The official spot to buy a t-shirt, koozie, keychain, hat, poster ... whatever the band manager thinks you cheap fans will want to buy as a momento for this extra-special weekend, this is the place to find it. This is high-quality – and high-price tag – stuff. By all means, you came, you saw, you got a t-shirt, but go easy here. There are infinitely cooler souvenirs to be purchased on Shakedown Street.

***merry pranksters*** An honorable reference to author Ken Kesey's crew in the 1960s who drove around in a psychedelic school bus and frequently dosed people with acid. Read Tom Wolfe's "Electric Kool-Aid Acid Test" for reference and for joy. To avoid run-ins with The

Establishment, you can dose people with joy instead of acid, ***just sayin'***. *See also:* ***6 Up!***

***Mind blown*** Woah.

***motherload*** The type of load that must be honored once a year with a present and called on a regular basis as long as it is alive

***Mr. Money Bags*** The guy on the Monopoly game. *See also:* ***VIP***

***music is the priority*** If you learn nothing else from this super-informative, educational and otherwise joke of a guide, learn this: At music festivals, MUSIC is the most important thing. You can get sidetracked with giggling in a corner with your friends and create wonderful memories, but I'm here to tell you: You do not have to pay $300 to do that. But front row at the Allman Brothers before Gregg died? That time Michael Franti and a fan danced on their hands in handstands on stage? Getting on stage at Dumpstaphunk? These are experiences that we'll never forget that are centered on music. Whatever you do, plan or think at a music festival, by all means, remember that MUSIC is why we are here.

## *N*

***new reality*** Coined by us after hearing endless talking heads say "new economy," the new reality is the mind-expanding concept of transcending all boundaries, including space and time, whether or not you can make a grilled cheese over an open fire and living in a world where you would rather hug people than not. Some may consider this a science fiction term, but those people would be kinda nerdy already. Or maybe there's a reader who thinks it's new age-y? Well, get ready, reader. Someone on this writing team is a Reiki master. The energy of the new reality is about to rock your world. *(EDIT: Cue the song: Age of Aquarius, OK, stop that. That's not a really good song.)*

***newbs*** Short for "newbie," or "new person" on the scene. Also spelled "noob." Inexperienced, unprepared, but stoked nonetheless, and there's something to be said for that. We were all newbs once, right kids? Of course, there's something derogatory in the connation of this term, like calling someone a dweeb. You gotta earn your stripes. *See also, **#sorrynotsorry***

***no energy is wasted*** This may or may not be associated with Newton's natural laws, but we think this is important for day-to-day living. Whatever you put energy to, you will find some sort of progress or change. So figure out where you wish to send your energy. Do you want to put energy toward worrying or complaining? Or do you want to put energy toward making new friends? Remember, time and space are actually illusions. Take control!

***no problem mon*** Heeeeeeeyyyyy mon! No worries. (Edit: Insert a ***shaka*** here, bro.)

## *O*

***One Show at a Time*** The honorable mantra and slogan on a sticker that "Wharf Rats," or sober ***heads,*** wear and proclaim at shows. Look, it is absolutely true that you do not need to drink or do drugs at a festival to have a good time. Why, you ask? Because ***music is the priority***. It's not a "drug festival," it's a music festival. We're all here to smile and dance in a crowd to bands we love. And if you need the support of your fellow Wharf Rats to keep your life together while seeing live music, then we absolutely support you. We do not want you to ruin your life because your festy vices are messing with you. The whole point of this Fest Life Guide is to make having fun sustainable. Addiction is not sustainable. If you have a problem with drugs or alcohol, seriously, we support you getting help so you can rage on in a longer-term fashion.

***one unopened bottle of water per person*** This bottle can be as big as a gallon, if not exactly stated in the rules. UNOPENED. Stash it with a friend who is vending, and fill up your water bottle or Camelbak throughout the day.

***Operation Big Fun*** What do we want? BIG FUN! When do we want it? NOW! (*EDIT: The writing team is feeling pent up and there's still a ways to go to complete this glossary ... oh my God, they're singing and playing "Girls Just Want To Have Fun" on the ukulele instead of writing again. Ahhh!)* As a festival participant, your goal to bring as many contagious smiles to your friends and everyone around you. You're not here to have a crummy time. You're here for Operation Big Fun!

## *P*

***Paranoia Will Destroy Ya!*** Said with the same melody as the Twilight Zone theme song, this important mantra must be repeated if you have a tendency to think the world is out to get you. There is a fine balance that must be created between paranoia and ***Constant Vigilance***. We personally tend to err on the side of vigilance and decide that the Universe loves us endlessly so, like, chill out. But that doesn't mean we're stupidheads.

***Party pants*** Pull up those flowery, tie-dye pants, baby. It's going to be a funky ride!

***people-watching*** Hey, look at that guy. Hey, look at her! Look over there! And repeat. This has the potential to be an all-day activity, perfect for healing hangovers, resting bodies and generally basking in otherwise braindead states of consciousness. No need to be a showboat all the time – but then ... *see also:* ***You make it happen***

***perma-grin*** A grin that is permanent. One of those "You better wipe that silly grin off yer face, boy!" kind of shit-eating smiles where you look around and everything is *soooooo* great, but you're totally serious! *Ahhhh..., perma-grin. See also,* ***cupcakes***

***personal "business" card*** A small piece of cardstock with your name, contact information and any beautiful bit of art or blessings you'd wish to give the recipient. These can be handmade or purchased for cheap, designed in any way that you wish someone to remember you by

***phamily*** Specific to Phish heads friends who are your ride-or-dies. See also: ***framily***

***phat cats*** While it is true that phat cats often have excess cash, this isn't really about economic status. Phat cats, in regards to a music festival, are those really rotund men (99 percent of the time) who love nothing more than to don an apron and stand over a grill all festival. They love serving food, eating food, watching you eat the food they prepare. It's a big deal, food. For phat cats, food is their identity. You've got to honor that, even if they are just heart attacks waiting to happen. They've packed their entire kitchen, so ask these fine folks if you need something. Vegetarians, beware. This is a meaty bunch. See also: ***festy foodies***

***picking up what I'm putting down*** If you do, you are understanding what I'm talking about.

***poi*** Toys that frequently glow with LED lights or are set on fire and then spun around in a flowing motion. Traditionally, poi are two orbs attached to chains of sorts that are spun in mesmerizing fashion. Poi can also be a description for a "dragon staff" or hula hoop that is lit on fire and spun about.

***prefer to hug*** The common greeting at a music festival, but, in our opinion, not the first. The first thing that should be done culturally is to extend your hand for a handshake. Then, if the person says, "Naw! Come on in!," then at least you have set up the expectation that the initial how-do-you-do hug takes the place of a handshake. You can tell a lot about a person with their handshake, and it's not something to be taken lightly. Also, sometimes the person you are being introduced to is a creep. Just know there is an option that can still be quite nice and keeps them an arms-length away. We love hugs and prefer to hug the vast majority of the time, but not always.

***Print a copy*** Before you leave for the festival – in those days at work when you're staring at your computer but really imagining the fun you're about to have, print out the schedule on a couple pages that you can fold and stuff in a pocket. This is very important; do not presume that the festival organizers have their act together enough to print enough easily used and organized schedules. Frequently, these large color pamphlets contain lots of ads, barely discernable maps and weird blocky schedules. You cannot carry them on your person if you don't have a big bag, which comes with its own consequences. Trust us, be self-sufficient and come with a schedule AND a game plan.

## *Q*

## *R*

***rage stick*** Crowd art that is the subject of much debate in the festival scene: Some love 'em, some hate 'em. The haters are justifiably annoyed at the fact that these art-on-a-tall-stick that people carry in crowds can block the view of those behind. They are silly and often ***bizarro***. There can be way, way too many, and sometimes people just simply don't put much effort into them. This writing team loves 'em. We love that you can tell your friend, "We'll be near the glitter-covered blender on a stick" or "Just look for the unbelievably huge photo of Bill Murray's face on a stick and we'll be to the right." For a while, we thought this type of art was simply called "crowd art," but we were schooled and then loved how you could see the level of excitement and rage – in a good way – the holder was experiencing with the music based on the movement level of said stick. See also: ***let's rage!***

***Reefer Madness*** A cult classic movie from the 1930s in which a school principal warns parents to the dangers of marijuana, a "viscous plant" that is "rooted in hell" and results in "hopeless insanity." It's hilarious. Another example of this ridiculosity is the "Blue Boy" episode of Dragnet. Enjoy.

***Reiki*** Healing energy from the universe. You must be attuned to the Reiki energy in order to use it to facilitate healing in others. It is a wonderful healing tradition, and we are proud to be a part of it. You may think it's a bunch of baloney, but that's probably because you've simply never experienced it.

***riding the rail*** The "rail" of which we speak is the gate security teams put up to separate the crowd of hippies from the musical acts. First row for the general admission concert. There are a lot of nice benefits to "riding the rail," including: 1) No one to block your view, 2) A place to stash your bag where no one will walk over it, 3) A place to lean and 4) An immovable barrier that provides a sense of place that other people in the crowd recognize and honor. To accomplish this position, you have to act fast and slippery, moving into vacated spots ahead of you quickly and smoothly, so that you can maintain peace among the crowd while edging closer and closer to the front. This takes skill. Do not attempt if you are drunk, tall or oddly stationary when there's a major dance party erupting in the front.

***rope sandals*** Also known as "Jesus sandals." At Lock'n, we sold the SHIT out of those rope sandals with our friend Magoo, who owned the shop "Magoo's Hippie Stuff." However, Magoo will to this day claim that it was the popularity of the shoe and not our amazing merchandising and selling skills. Whatevs, Magoo! We also bought a pair for our Dad, and he loved them because they are super-comfy. You want a pair, don't you? Let us get your size. Oh my gosh, they fit perfectly! And they're only going to get MORE comfortable. Seriously. My dad has a pair and loves them. You wanna get 'em? Awesome! Let us ring you out.

## *S*

***STFU*** Shut The Funk Up. *See also:* ***The Golden Rule of Festival Crowds***

***set yourself up for success*** Get off your rump-shaker, dear reader. By reading this guide, you've hopefully figured out that you are able to create anything you want in life. That does not mean magical stuff will just fall out of clear air and land at your feet. No, you must make this happen for yourself. No energy is wasted. You need to lay the foundation of own your life in order to build what you envision. *See also:* ***do your future self a favor***

***shaka*** A hand sign originating from the surfer culture. To create, make a loose fist with your right hand and stick out your thumb and your pinkie. Not as common as music festivals as the peace sign, which is the pointer and middle fingers sticking up with the inner hand facing out. For all things holy, please do not attempt the backward or sideways peace sign, and say things like "deuces!" because we are all just shaking our collective head.
***Shakedown Street*** With origins dating back to simply the main strip of the Dead lot, it is now found in some capacity, sometimes a few of them, in every festival. This is where vendors of everything from tie-dyes, crystals, grilled cheese sandwiches, secondhand clothing, ***lot shirts***, yummy vegetable noodle concoctions, kombucha, beers and more set up shop. Get yer drugs here. Get yer everything here. But try not to get yer ya yas out, have a little decency. *See also* ***1 4 2 3 4 5*** *and* ***festy fashions***
***#Sorrynotsorry*** This is a flip way of saying: We simply do not care that your feelings were hurt because the entire universe is on our side here. We added the hashtag because it was, like, so young and hip!
***spunions*** Late-night folks who have likely ingested some psychedelics recently who wander from camp site to camp site in search of adventure and interesting glittery things to be mesmerized by. Often underweight due to forgetting to eat. Usually harmless but have been known to go a little crazy, but only temporarily, we swear. *See also: first light early birds*
***stalker-style white van*** Cue the *Jaws* theme song. However, lots of cool people, for utilitarian reasons, purchase these types of vehicles. Our buddy Magoo had one, and so did Jasper, the amazing artist who projected lights and far-out videos on trees and huge screens. So,

when meeting someone with one of these, often-windowless vehicles, it's either going to go really well, or really, really bad.

## *T*

***tie-dye onesies*** Some people think it's cute to put babies in little clip on ties and, "*ahhh, it's the little executive!*" Not this writing team. No, we are quite partial to slapping some crazy swirling colors on people and letting them figure out how to work the parts of their bodies and search for the boob. Just keep the kids away from the fruity craft beers, OK?

***"There's live music happening!"*** Attention! Attention! We have an announcement to make! While you are all plopped around, there is a performance happening that will never happen again! Don't miss it! Look, at music festivals, there are always going to be people hanging around the campfire. These people are probably drinking, laughing, smoking weed, playing music themselves, eating and talking about things they need to do, like take a hippie shower or at least change this stinking shirt, man. It is very easy to get wrapped up in this camp scene. You love these people. We know, this is the crew. But let's talk about what's important here. Hint: It's not whether Jonathan is going to finish that entire bag of Lays Potato Chips. Focus on the end game, people. Get to the show. See also: ***music is the priority***

***The bigger the dreadlocks, the tastier the grub***. This universal rule is a good way to determine the stand from which you will purchase your take-away food at a music festival. Usually, Rastas will add just a little bit of love to every dish! (Plus, there will surely be a vegetarian option.)

*See also: Parliament Funkadelic's line, "The bigger the headache, the bigger the pill, baby."*

***"The man can't keep me down!"*** And that's the truth!!

***ticket high*** *starts scratching arms* Hey, hey man. You got any of them, um, you know. *eyes shift back and forth* tickets? 'Cause, um, you know, we're really up for, like, dancing around our living rooms in our pajamas, smiling widely and doing little shimmies, calling our friends and posting updates on social media about our awesomely fun plans we just created for ourselves. You want how much? Just put it on the credit card, dude. See also: ***perma-grin***

***trade blanket*** A wonderful, interactive festival activity. Lay out any old blanket or tapestry and sprinkle random things on it: a condom, some candy, maybe even a few mystery items wrapped up with a big question mark on it. In order to take something, you must leave something. Signage is helpful.

***travel as a family*** When a group of friends stick together. Friends who dance together, stay together. It's nice to travel as a family, because then you won't spend any precious time tracking down your pals to enjoy the show together. But sometimes this can be a drag, especially if you're the black sheep of your family. Some people want to look at stuff on Shakedown Street, stand in long lines for cheap beer or stay in a bad location in a crowd. It's OK to break from the family and go out on your own. Don't worry, we still love you. *See also:* ***framily***

***trust your instinct*** ALWAYS! Always listen to that little voice inside you. It is correct. Think maybe that dude isn't selling what he's claiming to sell? Don't buy it. Think going down that path is a bad idea? Don't go down that path. Think someone is a creep? Don't hang out with that person. Always, always, honor yourself and what you know to be right.

***Two wrongs don't make a right*** Learned everything you needed to know in kindergarten, eh? Then why do you think it's OK to be a jerk to a jerk? That's not the solution. That's not the way to achieve success in ***Operation Big Fun***. But do two rights make a left? No, then you're going backwards. Think about it. We didn't.

## *U*

***Universe provides*** You have to conspire with the universe. Do not make the universe your enemy. If it seems like things aren't going your way, wait a little while and you may recognize how necessary that perceived setback really was for your life and how far you've come. You must believe that you will be provided for, all the time, for what you need. Now, perhaps what you need and what you want don't jive? What a bummer. Wah-wahhh.

## *V*

***VIP*** High-roller territory here! These very important people spend a lot of money to get all kinds of perks at a festival, from food and drinks to clean flush toilets to a closer spot in the crowd. Festival promoters are increasingly creative in the up-sell of tickets, to make people spent more of their hard-earned cash. We've never done VIP because we know how to have an excellent time without having to fork over the coin. But if you've got the bucks and want to splurge, have at it. We don't fault you one bit. *See also:* ***Mr. Money Bags***

## *W*

***wear a watch*** One year, we neglected to bring a watch with us and never knew when it was time to leave one stage to head over to catch the band we were very excited to see. We were at a disadvantage until we stumbled upon Short Cut Camp's trade blanket. And there was a little, cheap cartoon-covered digital watch. We had a piece of jasper. We put it down on the blanket. We strapped on that watch. Party on.

***Whatever you do, take care of your shoes*** No truer words spoken, thank you Phish.

***"What happened?"*** Our grandmother's response to questions such as "Could you please pass the salt?" and "I love you!" Feel free to co-op, especially to police officers.

***wookie (or wook, for short)*** Named after the furry Star Wars characters, these are young hippie types with unkempt hair, often with pitbulls, who they're always not particularly nice to. This fascinating hippie subculture dresses in dark colors, enlarge the holes in their ears, sleep in vans, are a little aggressive, drink heavily and are communal in nature. They are known to steal and can be fantastic in bed, not that anyone in this writing group would even dream! Why, we'd neva! (*Edit: Oh yes you would.)*

***wook flu*** The crummy sickness one gets upon returning from a music festival. We've heard (*cough cough*) that the sure-fire way to avoid the wook flu is to kiss a wook. Look, um, we just heard it. It's not like all our friends who partied with us at the not-to-be-named festival got deathly sick with the flu immediately upon return and we didn't. What? We have really healthy immune systems and lived by the ***Golden Rule.*** We swear, it had nothing to do with the fact that we kissed a boy with dirty dreadlocks and this interesting tattoo of meteors flying into space.

***working vacation*** File under "Dat don't make no sense." Figuring out a way to make money while enjoying a music festival – or any getaway – takes ingenuity, creativity and tenacity. We honor those traits. But if you want to really relax, disconnect. Turn off the cell phone. Don't work. Play! There is a lack of play in the world, because by attending school for more than a decade of our life we are conditioned institutionally to believe that work is valued but playtime is for kids. Well, we aren't ashamed of being kids at heart.

## X

## Y

***You can't do everything*** You have to figure out what you want to do. What is most important to you? Not everyone arrives at a music festival with the end game in mind; in order to maximize ***Operation Big Fun***, you must. Which bands do you want to see? When are they? What are you going to eat before or after that show? Think it out. Because you'll unfortunately have to miss a few things that you really, really wished you could have done or seen. It's the nature of the beast so chill out and do the best you can.

***You don't have to do them all*** And by them, we mean drugs. Yes, in the glossary entry above, you may think that we are encouraging you to do as much as you possibly can. But not drugs. We do not encourage that. Why? Because when you do too many drugs, you mess up your night because you can't keep your shit together and you forget what band played and your cognitive dissidence is so acute that you may become a liability to your friends and everyone around you. It is never a good idea to mix your drugs. When (and if) you are partaking in illegal substances, be smart about it. Figure out what you want to do, when, with whom ... prepare yourself for what you are about to do. You owe it to yourself. Don't let social pressure impact you in anyway. We mean, who taught you how to do this stuff? (*EDIT: Insert picture of brain-on-drugs fried egg here.)*

***you have the time*** We're all busy little bees, aren't we? Life is so crazy, between work and plans and plopping around on your sofa staring at social media. At music festivals, we are able to share our precious time with people we love. Give the gift of time. It's free. It's beautiful. *See also:* ***No energy is wasted.***

***your jam*** Used in a sentence: "Yo! Dats Ma JAM!" This phrase captures your enjoyment and perceived unique appropriation of a certain thing, be it a particular song to throwing ***glow sticks*** right on time to chowing down on a ***Jerry Roll.*** Anything you really like, dats your jam, sis.

***You make it happen*** We are excited to share with you: YOU CREATE YOUR OWN REALITY! That's right, you are 100% responsible for the life that exists around you. We know, we know ... you've been blaming that guy or your mom or your neighborhood or your skin color or whatever, but we're not sorry to tell you that it's all an excuse that is simply limiting your amazing ability to do whatever you want to do for the benefit of you and everyone around you. Congratulations! You are a major part of a festival experience, and we are so glad you're here! (*Edit: Hug time.*)

***You snooze you lose*** A proven fact originating from third grade, if you are a space cadet and someone jumps in front of you, tough noogies for you, buttercup. If someone grabs a seat while you twiddle your thumbs, wah-wahhhh. Five up high, five down low, five in the middle, whoops you're too slow, or some annoying weird game like that. See also: ***Don't be a jerk***

***yucks*** Ha ha! We think this is a Three Stoogs allusion, to which we hang our heads.

## Z

# 0-1 MILLION

***1 4 2 3 4 5*** Sigh! Really? We have to explain friggin' EVERYTHING to you? Ok, right, this is a guide. That's the whole point. Sorry. This means, "One beer and/or water, depending on what I'm holding in my hand, for two dollars, or you can purchase three of these fine quality and hopefully cold beverages for five dollars, thus saving an entire dollar, which can come in handy if you want to hook your friends up, and besides, you won't do better inside the venue, that's for damn sure. And I'm really trying to move all these beverages as fast as possible before I get busted." See also: ***6 UP***

***6 UP*** This is what you yell if you are a hippie in a crowd and you see a police officer. Be sure you are not doing anything wrong. Be sure you will not be seen directly yelling by said police officer. But warn your friends and heed the warning of others. Nobody likes getting busted. Origins of this saying are unknown, although it may relate to the position of the "6" on a clock face: aka "Turn around." A great T-shirt reads, "6-Up, the Uncoola." *See also:* ***lot shirts***

## ABOUT THE AUTHOR:

A professional writer for 20 years, Suzanne Wentley loves live music, meeting new people, having epic adventures and helping others be the very best they can be. Check out her website, *www.thelovelightproject.com*.